ATHLONE
MISCELLANY

ATHLONE
MISCELLANY

Gearoid O'Brien

The
History
Press
Ireland

First published 2011

The History Press Ireland
119 Lower Baggot Street
Dublin 2
Ireland
www.thehistorypress.ie

© Gearoid O'Brien, 2011

British Library Cataloguing in Publication Data.
A catalogue record for this book is available from the British Library.

ISBN 978 1 84588 709 4

Typesetting and origination by The History Press
Printed in Great Britain
Manufacturing managed by Jellyfish Print Solutions Ltd

Contents

Acknowledgements

First and foremost, I want to acknowledge my indebtedness to my wife, Angela Hanley, who is my Alpha and my Omega. We came together through our shared interest in writing, and out of that love blossomed. She has always been patient and understanding when the pressures of producing a weekly article (added to the pressures of work) became too much for me. It is wonderful to have such a friend. I am truly blessed.

I have two adult children – they have each enriched my life in countless ways. They too have their talents and use them wisely. At different times and in different ways they have been inspirational, and for this I am grateful.

Since I started writing this column in January 1990, I have enjoyed the friendship and support of several people: Margaret Grennan, then editor of the *Westmeath Independent*, invited me to contribute the first articles, and to her I am still very grateful; Nicholas Nally, as managing director, was also extremely supportive, as was his son Martin Nally when he filled that same role. When Margaret Grennan stood down from her editorial role she was succeeded by Dave O'Connell and he too was an enthusiastic supporter of the column. Often, when I was flagging, a word from the editor ensured that the column continued to appear. By the time Tadhg Carey took over the editorship of the paper, I thought that the column had perhaps run its course. I thought that he might want to put his own stamp on the paper and that

Acknowledgements

I might perhaps bow out gracefully. But from early on, Tadhg made it clear that as long as I was prepared to write the column, he was more than happy to publish it. My relationships with all three editors have been excellent, and I wish to thank them individually and collectively.

A telephone call from The History Press led to this book being compiled. To my publisher Ronan Colgan and to Finbar Jordan (a fellow past pupil of St Aloysius College) who set this project in motion, I am most grateful. It would have been very embarrassing, after twenty years, to try to find yet another excuse as to why a selection of these pieces had not found its way into print.

To all my colleagues in Westmeath County Library Service and to all those in the *Westmeath Independent* who have answered phones, set the type or extended courtesies to me over the years, a heartfelt thank you. I am also most grateful to the photographers of Athlone, past and present, including Ann Hennessy and P.J. Murray in particular, who have always been more than generous with their photographs.

And last but not least to you, the reader, a hundred thousand thanks. Your letters, phone calls, emails and support over the course of twenty years has ensured that I now hold the record for the longest-running local history column. Without your encouragement I might have thrown in the towel many years ago. I hope that you will enjoy this compilation of some two dozen articles from the more than 1,000 published to date.

Gearoid O'Brien

Foreword

Regional newspapers, by their very nature, deal with the minutiae of daily existence in their circulation areas.

Often they tend to be parochial, in the best spirit of that word. Life in all its rich variety, and indeed death, is captured in their columns. Their world horizons are restricted to their circulation hinterland. If all politics is local, all news is local for a regional newspaper. Many of these newspapers also tend to have served their communities over generations. The *Westmeath Independent* in Athlone, of which I am editor, has been published since 1846.

All of this combines to ensure local newspapers are invaluable local history resources and fantastic archives for genealogical or other researchers. However, in Athlone, the *Westmeath Independent* has a keen rival. Here there is another priceless local history resource, in the person of town librarian and author Gearoid O'Brien.

Gearoid's unparalleled, almost encyclopaedic knowledge of the town, its people, its environs and its history is truly remarkable. More importantly, it is accompanied by a generosity of spirit which knows no bounds. He is the ultimate go-to man for local history queries; no question is ever too mundane or too time consuming for him to answer. In his role as town librarian, and as *de facto* town historian, it is no exaggeration to say he has helped thousands of people with local heritage and genealogy queries. In turn, these queries – and the often complicated and detailed research he undertakes in order to assist the public – have served only to deepen his own knowledge of the town.

As editor of the *Westmeath Independent*, where his 'Athlone Miscellany' column has appeared for over twenty years, I, more than most, am familiar with the value of Gearoid's local history writings. There has always been healthy public feedback to his columns, often from remote corners of the world, where descendants of Athlonians of yesteryear reside. The warmth, respect and esteem which Gearoid O'Brien and his 'Athlone Miscellany' columns elicit have always been clearly evident. For that reason, the *Westmeath Independent* is delighted to welcome the publication of a selection of 'Athlone Miscellany' columns in this fine volume. It can only serve to further satisfy a growing band of local-history devotees.

For those for whom this is a first encounter with the 'Athlone Miscellany' series, the pieces contained herein are a suitably varied selection and a fine taster for the larger series. Over the 1,000-plus 'Athlone Miscellany' columns which have graced the pages of the *Westmeath Independent*, what is most evident is the depth and breadth of knowledge and the intensity of the research required in their preparation.

But these columns are not self-indulgent whimsies. Not only are they, as I have outlined, warmly received by the general public, they are often inspired by suggestions from readers. The content may be diverse and wide ranging – or as the label says, miscellaneous – but that does not mean it is any way random or disconnected. On topics as varied as the history of a local church to a sensational court case over an unfulfilled marriage proposal, there is a common thread. These columns are all rooted in their locality. They are of Athlone and for Athlone. And they all serve to further our collective knowledge of Athlone and its environs.

Many of the miscellany columns are part of longer series and are thus unsuitable for a collection of individual columns such as this. That, however, does not lessen their importance. The series of pieces on the history of one of Athlone's oldest streets, Connaught Street, is a marvellous piece of local research. These articles moved from the macro to the micro level, shifting from an initial overview of the street to a detailed examination of the history of each individual property. In its own way, the Connaught Street series could be described as a local history version of Google's Street View, as it allows the reader to zoom in on individual homes on the street and watch as their inhabitants change over time.

In their own way, the twenty years of 'Athlone Miscellany' columns also represent the foremost attempt at a directory of biography of Athlone's most prominent figures. There you will find the life stories of the great, the good, the notorious and the infamous. And Gearoid O'Brien's keen eye for that nugget of historical value is an ever-present constant. Throughout, O'Brien brings a rigorous attention to detail and a distinctive enthusiasm to bear on his subject matter.

Many of the columns are also a tribute to O'Brien's ability to put interviewees and sources at their ease in order to elicit important information. A series of columns based on the folk memory of the late Jimmy O'Connor, one of the town's older residents, is, for example, a model of its type.

Over its twenty-year history, 'Athlone Miscellany' has become a permanent feature of the local media landscape and has etched a niche in the affections of thousands of people, from this region and further afield. It is my hope that this particular publication will serve not only to shine attention on the series itself, but also have a similarly long-lasting impact on its readers.

Tadhg Carey
Editor
Westmeath Independent

1

Aspects of Military Life in Athlone in the Eighteenth Century[1]

The recent commemoration of the seventy-fifth anniversary of the takeover of the military barracks in Athlone has helped to focus attention on the history of this venerable institution. It serves also as a timely reminder that we will soon be in a position to commemorate an Irish record – 300 years of continuous military presence in an Irish military barracks. In the past I have written at considerable length about the history of the military in Athlone, but I feel it may be useful to gather together some fugitive facts and accounts which throw further light on the early history of the barracks.

With the growth of newspapers in the eighteenth century, a few interesting snippets survive from the 1730s. Some do little more than to cite a name, while others give clues to the regiments which were stationed in Athlone at that particular time. In September 1732, we learn that the Hon. Colonel William Egerton was in charge of a Regiment of Foot stationed in Athlone. The following year, 1734, saw two cases of desertion which made the national press. In May, one Hugh Weir, aged about fifty, deserted from Major Hamilton's troop of Colonel Bowle's regiment of dragoons, while in August a reward of £4 was offered for the 'apprehension of Hugh Henderson, a deserter of Captain Alexander Burnet's company in Sir James Wood's regiment of foot' then stationed in Athlone.

Engraving of Athlone Castle.

Further Desertions

In January 1734, two further cases of desertion were reported: one concerned John Coughlan, a drummer with Lord Molesworth's troop of dragoons, and the other a corporal called Joseph Thames, who deserted from Captain Alexander Burnet's company of the regiment of North British Fusiliers, then quartered in Athlone.

The earliest description we have of a deserter refers to William Ferguson, who deserted his regiment in September 1740. He belonged to Colonel St George's regiment of dragoons, was aged thirty-two years, was six feet tall, and his face was marked by smallpox. He wore a blue cloth coat with scarlet lining and brass carved buttons, a yellow waistcoat and blue cloth breeches. One would have imagined that he might stand out in a crowd!

Army Celebrate Victory in Germany

A newspaper report of 5 July 1743 claims:

> We hear from Athlone that on Sunday last after they received
> the account of His Majesty's glorious victory in Germany
> the Hon. Lieutenant Thomas Darby, who commands a troop
> of dragoons in that Corporation, marched the troops into
> the streets at about 2 o'clock at night, at which time the
> post came in and fired three volleys which were answered by
> the militia of the Corporation. The town was immediately
> illuminated and bonfires erected in several parts of the town
> but it was too late for the bells to be rung and to drink the
> health requisite upon the occasion … the next day … sev-
> eral of the toasts were drunk by the Corporation in general,
> all of whom assembled together at the 'Three Blackamoors'
> on the occasion.

In December 1747, a reward was offered for the capture of
Charles Ormsby, who deserted from Captain Francis Reynolds
troop of Major General De Grangine's regiment of dragoons
then stationed in Athlone Barracks.

The Trial of Lieutenant Tucker

In April 1749, an altercation broke out between two lieutenants,
resulting in the death of one of them. A Lieutenant Weekes (or
Reeves) was stabbed three times with a knife, causing injuries to
the 'belly, the breast and the throat'. Following a coroner's inquest,
which brought in a verdict of wilful murder, Lieutenant Tucker
was arrested and committed to Roscommon Gaol.

In August of that year, Lieutenant Tucker of General Blakeney's
regiment was tried at Roscommon Assizes for killing Lieutenant
Reeves (earlier report stated the names as Weekes). Following a

trial which lasted six hours, the jury acquitted Tucker, who had brought in the notion of manslaughter in his own defence.

Intent upon Destruction

On 12 February 1754, the papers reported, 'On last Sunday a soldier in Athlone attempted to throw himself over the Bridge but was prevented by some passers by. He afterwards cut his throat but not fatally. He then had recourse to his sword with which he stabbed himself in the breast.' Unfortunately we hear no more about this soldier and do not know whether the story had a happy outcome, but it is probably unlikely.

Desertions continued from Athlone Barracks, including that of Terence Malone, a soldier of the 2nd battalion of the 76th regiment of foot, commanded by Lord Forbes, who absconded in 'full regimentals' in October 1760 and for whom a £3 reward was offered. Three years later, in March 1763, seven soldiers of the 92nd regiment were sent to Roscommon to stand trial for the murder of Peter Keogh near Athlone a year earlier – sadly the paper did not report on the outcome of that trial.

The Twelfth of July

A report of 15 July 1769 shows that the 'Twelfth of July' was being celebrated in Athlone. The original report reads as follows:

The 12th July being the anniversary of the Battle of the Boyne where the glorious King William's forces obtained a decisive victory (a remarkable episode in the annals of liberty and independence in this kingdom). Thomas Cooke the active and vigilant vice-sovereign of the burgesses, bailiffs and freemen of Athlone with the insignia of this ancient corporation assembled at the Tholsel[2] and from thence walked in procession to the centre of the bridge where by a signal from the Tholsel bell they met five companies of the 50th Regiment commanded by Major General Sir William Boothby and proceeded then to the hill remarkable for being the place of encampment of King William's army and being there drawn up with the Corporation on the right, fired three excellent volleys and returned in the same order to the Three Blacks Inn[3] where they spent the evening together with a true spirit of loyalty, concord and generous zeal for the liberty and independence of the kingdom and where nothing was wanted but the presence of our truly worthy sovereign of Athlone Revd Dean Handcock (who was prevented from being present through indisposition). The night concluded with many loyal and patriotic toasts, bonfires, illuminations and other demonstrations of joy.

Notes

1 First published 1997.
2 The Tholsel, or Market House, was situated in Custume Place, facing towards Northgate Street. The site it occupied is now part of the public footpath leading from the town bridge towards Burgess's shop, where the Desmond Broe memorial to those who died for Irish freedom is located.
3 The Three Blackamoor's or The Three Blacks was an inn in Main Street, Athlone. It was the precursor of the present Sean's Bar.

2

J.M. Fallon, Apothecary and Postmaster

There were few more colourful or complex characters in nine-teenth-century Athlone than the local apothecary, sometime journalist and one-time postmaster, Joseph Malachy Fallon, who lived in what is now known as O'Connell Street. In Fallon's time, and with his connivance, it was renamed Wentworth Street, in honour of a senior government official of the day. Later, when Wentworth could no longer return any favours, he tried to have a plebiscite taken among the inhabitants of the street to rename it Mulgrave Street in honour of a successor of Wentworth's. When his bid to have the street name changed failed, he insisted on changing his own business address from Wellesley Medical Hall to Mulgrave Medical Hall and to adding Mulgrave Street to his address, although he was, clearly, the only resident using that address. The use of Mulgrave Street dated to 1837-38 and a typical advertisement of Fallon's at that time appeared in a local newspaper of 12 May 1837:

Mulgrave Medals

The Mulgrave Medal Committee has appointed Mr J.M. Fallon, State Apothecary, agent for the sale of Mulgrave Medals in Athlone where medals of any description from Fifteen Guineas down to two shillings and sixpence can be had.

Mulgrave Medical Hall, Mulgrave Street, Athlone.

Perhaps the most colourful episode in the life of Fallon was when he was postmaster and subjected to an inquiry for interfering with postal items. He entered into a spirited self-defence through the columns of the local press.

Athlone Post Office Inquiry

In September 1833, J.M. Fallon wrote a short letter to the editor of one of the local newspapers. It read:

> A paragraph is going the rounds of the papers, headed 'Post Office Investigation' in which my name has been unfairly treated. May I request you will state in your next [issue], by my authority, that the statement is false, inasmuch as no such charge of opening letters has been instituted.
>
> I remain, Sir, your obedient servant,
> J.M. Fallon.

I'm sure Fallon hoped that this denial would end the matter, but the local press, having none of the modern fears of libel laws, continued to speculate on the case. In a leading article in the *Roscommon Journal* in November 1833, the editor wrote:

> ### Mr Fallon, late Post Master of Athlone
>
> This gentleman, it appears, has taken himself to the 'inno-cent' and we should hope more harmless amusement of letter writing as opposed to that of letter reading; and if being well acquainted with the affairs of others be any acquisition he can well boast of such an acquisition. However before he involves himself in further difficulties we advise him to try and get rid of those with which he is surrounded and turn his vacuity to more beneficial purposes. His threat of proceedings against the

proprietor of the *Journal* is treated with its merited contempt; and to convince him we are friendly towards him and that we pity him in his misfortunes, we shall give him our advice which may be of some service hereafter. If he has money to sport on law, after he pays his just debts, he may do so, but if he has suspended over him such 'ill looking things as executions, etc.' we say settle them before you proceed further. With respect to the charges against Mr Marshall we think he should have justified his own conduct first before he ventured to impugn that of another. Such subterfuge must ultimately lead the public to discuss the merits of both – and as he is the aggressor people will naturally enquire first whether he deserved to be dismissed; and next whether such dismissal was grounded on a violation of those duties which he was sworn to discharge; and if they are satisfied on this point, then the attack on the character of Mr Marshall by a person so circumstanced will appear in no other light than that of ill-timed and invidious.

Fallon's Reply

Within days of the publication of this attack on Fallon's character he had retaliated with a reply which was printed in an Athlone paper of the day:

Dear Sir,
The *Roscommon Journal* has again indulged in its usual low Billingsgate style and in its attempt to be witty has only held forth the unfortunate writer to the contempt and pity that are generally bestowed on articles coming from such a genius; it is generally believed since the Roscommon Printing Office was set fire to *by accident* that the Proprietor was labouring under periodical aberrations of mind and never was it fully ascertained until the Printing Devil swore before the Grand Jury what led them to throw out the presentment so *ably* and

ingeniously sought for by the *innocent Proprietor*. Under these circumstances I freely forgive the poor Devil; with regard to the defence of the Deputy Sovereign it is surprising to me, if his worship ought not to be content with his mock requisition without the *ineffectual* assistance of a [?]. I shall offer one observation in conclusion as relates to myself *viz*. that I feel convinced from the character of the *lads* employed in my investigation that the whole plot was laid through the worst of party or political feeling for who can read the names of the select half-dozen without at once coming to the proper conclusion. However I shall say nothing but give them an advice at the next investigation they may want to swear; let them keep in mind the following words: Let them now swear who never swore before and those who always swear now swear the more. I regret so much trespassing on you but I feel convinced you will be ever ready to protect the innocent from the malicious attacks of a disappointed part. Believe me, dear Sir, Yours etc., Joseph M. Fallon.

A Successor is Appointed

According to the *Roscommon Journal* of 1 November 1833, Mr Fallon had been dismissed from the office of postmaster by order of his Grace, the Duke of Richmond, and that Mr W. Dean had been appointed to the position. It was also rumoured that the postmaster of Boyle had also been dismissed. The editorial stated:

> It is not our province, neither is it our nature, to exult in the misfortunes of any person, no matter how he may have been opposed to us – but this much we feel ourselves bound to say, that we trust the enquiry into Mr Fallon's conduct and the result will be a caution to other Postmasters, the negligence of some of whom is most culpable.

Later that month, an Athlone paper had an open letter from Fallon, addressed to 'the Merchants, Traders and Inhabitants of Athlone thanking them for their support'. In the course of the letter, he paid particular tribute to the local parliamentary representative, Mr Talbot. Fallon states, 'it gives me sincere pleasure to find he has got the appointment of my successor; he has made that appointment in the person of an honest and independent elector – but how confounded must the wretch be who expected himself to be appointed'. He concludes by thanking some of his 'old friends and school-fellows', Messrs Moore, Kelly and O'Connor, 'I return my most grateful acknowledgement for the trouble they took.'

The editor adds the final comment:

The editor regrets the departure of Mr Fallon – his obliging manner gained the good-will and approbation of the inhabitants of Athlone in general and ours in particular – he must have his faults – for who is without them? But we aver his are not the faults of the heart; one great consolation he has and one of which he may be justly proud, he resigns his trust with an untainted and unblemished character, a circumstance few, very few Post Masters in giving up their charge can boast of.

3

Eel Fishing: Athlone's Oldest Industry

The eel weirs in Athlone were a series of posts and nets stretching across the river from the docks towards the strand, with a pass on the Leinster side – traditionally called the Queen's Pass – to allow some fish to negotiate the river without being caught. These eel nets added greatly to the atmospheric look of the river in winter, and watching the boatman empty these nets into vats for transportation to the holding tank was a favourite pastime of some people. The eel fisheries were controlled by the ESB and the eels caught in Athlone were destined for the continental market.

It is impossible to say, with any degree of accuracy, when eel fishing first became a commercial activity in Athlone, but it seems likely that for as long as man has crossed the Shannon at this point, that eels have been fished for on some scale. Among the earliest documentary evidence for the history of Athlone, a town which grew up around an Anglo-Norman castle on the banks of the Shannon, are several references to the eel-fishing industry.

The Cluniac priory on the west bank of the Shannon predates the Anglo-Norman settlement of Athlone. According to tradition, the priory was established about the year AD 1150 under the patronage of Turlough O'Connor, King of Connaught. In the Calendar of Documents relating to Ireland, 1171-1251, there is a reference to the Priory of Sts Peter & Paul, Athlone, indicating that the castle (Athlone Castle) was built on land belonging to the monks of this priory in 1210. In August 1214, King John ordered Henry, Archbishop of Dublin, to give the monks of Athlone the tenth part of the expenses of the castle in exchange for their land, on which the castle was built. The prior was also given four cantreds of land in Loughsewdy (Ballymore) but these were subsequently restored to Walter de Lacy, their former owner.

The Eel Fisheries of Athlone

In 1216, the priory was once again mentioned in dispatches. Having been dispossessed of the land at Loughsewdy, the king ordered further compensation to be paid to the prior for the loss of its meadow, fishery and tithes. We know from the early records that the monks received an annuity of 'ten marks' per annum between 1235 and 1290. According to Archdall in *Monasticon Hibernicum*, published in 1786, Edward I granted the 'weirs and fisheries' of Athlone to St Peter's Abbey. These fisheries were to be the cause of much aggravation over the years. In 1284, the monks complained to the Crown that the Justiciar, Archbishop Stephen de Fulborn, had constructed two mills on the 'pool' which had injured their fisheries. The 'pool', which had previously yielded many eels, now yielded nothing. The king asked the Justiciar to ensure that his mills did not harm the monk's fisheries but apparently the problem continued unabated. In 1290, Prior Gilbert received 'forty shillings in silver' as compensation for the losses they had sustained in their 'pool' because of the polluting effect of the royal mill.

The fisheries were an important part of the commercial activity of Athlone. In 1286, 'the rent of pools and pontage of Athlone by the prior thereof' is shown in a roll of receipts for the Michaelmas term to amount to £15 6s 8d. The grant of the fisheries to the abbey was very important, because fish (and particularly eels) featured prominently in the diet of medieval Ireland. Tim O'Neill, in his excellent book *Merchants and Mariners in Medieval Ireland*, tells us that an Italian merchant living in Ireland, one Francesco Datini of Prato, who died in 1410, was very fond of eels. O'Neill states, 'he ate them pickled in their own fat with strong spices and wine or in a pie with spices, olive oil and orange and lemon juice'.

Thomas de Pykering was one of those who had weirs (or gurgites) at Athlone. In accounts for 30 July 1293, de Pykering accounted for the sum of £4 16s 'out of 3,600 eels sold at Athlone'. In 1344, the king committed to Henry Dillon 'the weir and fishery of Athlone', which was held by the Crown at a rent of £10 per annum.

The Franciscans

The Franciscans arrived in Athlone in the thirteenth century and settled on the eastern bank of the river. The jury is still out on the exact whereabouts of the first Franciscan settlement; one school of thought places it inside the medieval town walls (on the site soon to be occupied by the Radisson Hotel or portion of the Silverquay apartment complex), while others suggest that the church would have been 'without the walls', perhaps on the site later occupied by the abbey graveyard. It would seem that, unlike the Cluniacs, they were unable to get generous fishing rights at Athlone; instead they were granted the use of two eel weirs and two water mills – one at Kilmacuagh, near Creggan, and the other at Mullenmeehan near Ballymore. While the mills were clearly at a distance from the monastery, the two eel weirs may have been at Athlone.

The Dissolution of the Monasteries

After the Dissolution of the Monasteries, there was a lease (the details of which were recorded in the Fiants of Elizabeth) granted to Andrew Breteton and dated 27 June 1570. Under the terms of this lease, Breteton received the rights to 'the site of the house of the friars of Athlone, etc., and two fishing weirs on the River Shrynninge' for thirty years from the determination of the existing lease. Two months later, a lease was granted to Edmund O'Fallone, for twenty-one years, for 'an eel weir in the river Shynnen in Connaught', which was described as part of the possessions of the late monastery of St Peter. This same property was the subject of a further lease, dated 5 August 1578, but in this one the privileges of the President of Connaught in respect of the property were recited, 'The President of Connaught having the house of Athlone in keeping shall, two nights in each month, have the use of the weir, O'Fallon supplying nets, boats, poles and other necessaries.'

Eel Fisheries in the Sixteenth Century

In looking at transcripts of documents relating to the sixteenth and seventeenth centuries, it becomes very obvious that fishing at Athlone was a most important economic activity. When Edmund Waterhouse was created bailiff for the Shannon he was vested with both powers and responsibilities. One of the duties given to him was to survey the weirs along the course of the river and to remove those that were impeding navigation; an exception was made for the weirs of the 'manor and abbeys of Athlone'.

In 1583, Sir Lucas Dillon was granted, for a period of sixty years, property which included the house of the friars at Athlone and 'two weirs upon the River Shynen'. Seven other weirs were included in another lease, this time in favour of George Alexander, who was granted the property of the Cluniac Priory.

The President of Connaught, whose headquarters were situated in Athlone Castle, had, in addition to 'the manor of Athlone', 'the demesne and fishing thereof'.

Seventeenth-Century Eel Weirs

In the Calendar of Patent Rolls of James I, there is ample evidence of the great extent of the eel fisheries in Athlone. In a document dated 22 February 1619 there is a list of no fewer than twenty-two eel weirs at Athlone.

The great authority on eel fishing in Ireland was the late Dr Arthur Went. In an article about eel fishing in Athlone first published in the *Journal of the Royal Society of Antiquaries of Ireland* over fifty years ago, Went gives a complete transcript of the document in question and writes about the prefix 'carra' as used in the weir names. He tells us, 'The word *Carra* in all the names is probably derived from the Irish word 'cora' – a weir; *Carramore* being the large weir; *Carrabeg*, the small weir; *Carrahenry*, Henry's weir; *Carrahenry-Jones*, Henry Jones's weir, and *Carracormack*, Cormack's weir, etc.'

The following document relates to the ownership of weirs on the Shannon at Athlone in 1619. It is to be found in the Patent Rolls of James I and it is worth quoting in full, as it represents a most important grant of weirs and tells us much about the economic importance of eel fishing in seventeenth-century Athlone:

To John Coman of Athlone, merchant, Roscommon and Westmeath counties, or either of them. The weirs of Carraraghnes, Carraenvollan, Carrabeg, and Carramore, on the Shannon. To hold during the lives of Barn., Coman, John Waple, and Jane Coman, and the survivor of them; rent six large eels at Easter and five at Michaelmas, yearly. To Will Macgauley; the weir at Carrawendachoila, on the Shannon – to hold during the lives of the said Will., and of John and Edm. Macgauley, and the survivor of them; rent two large eels at Easter and Michaelmas, yearly. To Jennett Missett, widow; the weirs of Grenanmore, Carraprier, Carracoiagh and Carraberry on the Shannon – to hold during the natural lives of the said Jennett Missett, and of Edm. and Oliv. Jones,

gents, and the survivor of them; rent two large eels at Easter
and Michaelmas, by equal portions, yearly. To Tho. Rochford,
tanner; the weir called the new weir, otherwise Carranowe,
with the weirs Carraharlin, and Carrataghdeve otherwise
Cartawentooden, on the Shannon – to hold during the lives
of John and Tho. Waple and John Rochford, and the survivor of them; rent, six large eels at Easter and Michaelmas,
by equal portions yearly. To Tho. Dillon, gent.; the weir of
Carrarecloigh, on the Shannon – to hold during the lives of
Tho. Dillon, Jane, his wife, and Edm., Dillon, Fitz William,
merch.; and the survivor of them; rent, six large eels, etc., as in
preceding. To Phil. Elder, fisherman; the weirs of Carralacken
and Carranegan on the Shannon – to hold during then lives
of said Phil. and of Will. McGauly, fisherman, and John Elder,
and the survivor of them; rent, two large eels at Easter and one
at Michaelmas, yearly. To Samuel Lovelock, gent., the weirs
of Carragarr, on the Shannon – to hold during the lives of
said Samuel, and Elinor, his wife, and the survivor of them;
rent, two large eels, etc., as before. To John Awbrey, gent.; the
weir of Carrahenry, on the Shannon – to hold during the
lives of Hen., Tho., and Any Awbrey, and to the survivor of
them; rent, two large eels, &c., as before. To Will. McGauly,
fisherman; the weirs of Carratowne otherwise Carraentoime,
on the Shannon – to hold during the lives of the said Will.,
and Marg., his wife and John McGauly, and the survivors of
them; rent two large eels, etc., as in preceding. To Tho. Waple,
junr., merch,; the weir of Carrabor, on the Shannon – to hold
during the lives of the said Tho., and of John Waple, and Tho.
Rochford, merch., and the survivor of them; rent six large eels
at Easter and Michaelmas, by equal portions, yearly. To Tho.
Athy, merch.; the weirs of Learbegg and Carrahenry-Jones on
the Shannon, in said co.s or either of them, – to hold during
the lives of said Thomas, Elinor, his wife and Edm., his son,
and the survivor of them; rent, eight large eels, etc., as before.
To Peter Fallon, the weir of Carramore, on the Shannon – to

hold during the lives of the said Peter, and of Fra., and Peter, his sons, and the survivor of them; rent, 6 large eels, etc., as before. To John Cliff, gent.; the weir of Carracormack, on the Shannon – to hold during the lives of Nich., Skinner, Christ. Jones and Peter Fallon, junr., merch., and the survivor of them; rent six large eels, etc., as before …

The people mentioned in the leases above represent some of the best-known merchant families in seventeenth-century Athlone. John Coman, the first mentioned, was one of the members returned to Parliament for Athlone in 1634-5. He may have been a Catholic. Waple and Awdrey were obviously new 'English' settlers who served on the Common Council around 1623, and names such as Dillon and McGauly are representative of the major Anglo-Norman and Gaelic families in the hinterland of Athlone.

Nineteenth-Century Eel Fisheries

In Isaac Weld's *Statistical Survey of the County of Roscommon* (Dublin, 1832, p.154), the author mentions the state of the eel fisheries, confirming that Athlone was a great source of eels for the Dublin market. It is interesting to note that Weld describes the type of eel weirs which were to disappear within ten years or so during the course of the Shannon Navigation works of the 1840s. He records:

The river here is deformed by numerous weirs constructed of wicker work and stakes, that appear some feet above the surface, for the purpose of catching eels, which abound in all parts of the Shannon. Vast quantities are occasionally taken after the autumnal and the first winter floods, which are deposited in reservoirs, and thence dealt out by the proprietors according to the demand. The Dublin market is largely supplied from this source.

The Old Eel House prior to demolition. (Courtesy of P.J. Murray, photographer, Athlone)

From very early on in the history of eel fisheries, it was known that eels could be kept alive for long periods in 'live boxes' submerged in a river or stream. On Lough Ree, and indeed on other lakes where islanders depended on the bounty of the lake for their livelihood, fishermen were known to fish 'out of season' and preserve their catch in fresh-water ponds on the islands.

Dr Went, in his pioneering article on the history of eel fishing in Athlone, quotes from a book written under the *nom de plume* 'A Cosmopolite' called *The Sportsman in Ireland*. The book was published in 1840 and describes the author's recent visit to Athlone in the company of his manservant, Owen. He sent Owen to seek out lodgings for them both, and when Owen returned, his master recorded his observations, some of which are very relevant on the subject of eels:

> There were, indeed, eels – and in such abundance, exposed at every shop, whiskey-hovel, or lodging window – eels of three,

The eel nets at Athlone. (Courtesy of P.J. Murray, photographer, Athlone)

four or five pounds, which would seem to imply that they constituted the chief food of the people. This turned out to be the fact. These animals descend the Shannon in such multitudes, that, in the autumn, after the flood, the rapids and falls in the narrow part of the river need only be crossed by a purse net, and tons worth of eels are taken in one night. Although throughout Kerry, I could never prevail on the people to cook much less eat them – at Athlone, if one may judge from the abundant display, they are in the highest repute.

The Shannon Navigation Works

In *The Second Report of the Commissioners for the Improvement of the River Shannon*, published in 1837, the Commissioners signalled the need to remove all impediments to navigation from the riverbed, including the eel weirs that proliferated at Athlone. They stated:

The removal of eel weirs might be considered as depriving the country of a valuable source of food and useful industry, but there can be no doubt that other modes of fishing for this prolific article, which will not be injurious to the navigation or drainage, will be discovered and practised; and we ourselves are making researches for such as may be at present exercised in other countries in order to have them introduced immediately on the removal of the existing weirs.

In the summer of 1849, during the course of the Shannon Navigation works, it was found necessary to erect a dam 'nearly opposite the Royal School, at the narrow part of the river', thus enabling horses and carts, together with teams of workers, to work on the riverbed. This dam was obviously quite close to the Ranelagh School, around the site of the old No.1 Battery. Members of the Athlone Sub-Aqua Club have told me that they have come across the evidence of this dam. Among the impediments removed from the riverbed were shoals, eel weirs and the remains of the Elizabethan bridge.

The Present Arrangement

Dr Went described the eel fishery at Athlone as it was in 1949 and over fifty years later it is largely unchanged:

> Immediately above the weir used for regulating the water level at Athlone a number of poles were driven into the bed of the river and on those coghill nets were fished ... Instead of a definite weir, fishing has been carried on from a simple structure consisting of a number of posts, suitably supported at intervals by vertical steel girders. Each fishing unit consists, apart from the vertical supporting girders, of two vertical posts firmly driven into the river bed ... these posts, called weir posts, are usually four to five inches in diameter. Alongside each post is a vertical iron-bar, known as the hinge ... These two pairs of posts and bars constitute in legal parlance 'a gap' in which a fishing net called a coghill net is fished.

Eels 'run towards the sea' in winter, usually between the last quarter and the first quarter of the moon from September to January, when even the moonlight is at its weakest, and it is therefore at this time of the year that the nets are set. The netting of eels is a night-time activity and consequently many people who don't find themselves down by the Shannon at late evening or early morning, during the dreary days of winter, are blatantly unaware of the extent of the eel fisheries of Athlone.

4

The Melias: A Character and a History Maker

It was Michael Kilkelly, writing in the *Westmeath Independent* about seventy years ago, who first recorded his impressions of an old Athlone character called Andy Melia. This was a time when every town in Ireland had its own characters – people who were witty or eccentric, or both. These characters are usually recalled in local lore through stories and anecdotes, some of which may well be apocryphal.

Andy Melia, who lived on Abbey Lane West, was a born wit, a mimic and practical joker without whom no town gallery would seem complete. He was well known for his role as a comedian in many of the local amateur theatrical productions and was also a comic dancer and singer. In the 1960s, the late Mr James Galvin of Connaught Street recalled seeing Andy perform a hilarious sketch in which he impersonated the dual characters of male and female at the same time, wearing a costume which was constructed so as to seem alternatively man and woman simply by changing sides.

Among the stories I have heard about Andy Melia was one about an occasion when there was a Protestant funeral in St Peter's graveyard, off King Street (now Pearse Street), a place colloquially known as Bully's Acre. Andy had climbed a tree to view the proceedings without being seen, but during the funeral the preacher said, 'I hear a voice from Heaven …' Andy couldn't resist the temptation and from his lofty perch he responded, 'Well I'm up here and I don't hear it.'

Fr O'Reilly & the Offerings

Fr Martin O'Reilly PP of St Peter's, who was an uncle of the Lysters, was keen on introducing funeral offerings, which were already traditionally collected at rural funerals. On one occasion, he called Andy Melia and gave him a half-crown and a sixpence for himself. A funeral was due to take place from Connaught Street the following day and Fr O'Reilly asked Andy to set an example by placing the half-crown on a table outside the house so that others, seeing what Andy had done, would do likewise. However, that night Andy spent the half-crown in a pub, treating himself and his friends at Fr O'Reilly's expense. He told all and sundry how and why he had got the money. The next afternoon at three o'clock, when the corpse was put out the window and the coffin was waiting, supported on two planks from Lyster's, Fr O'Reilly started reciting the prayers. He kept looking up at Andy and beckoning him but Andy didn't respond. Eventually Andy turned his pockets inside out to indicate that they were empty. All those in the know were greatly amused, but Fr O'Reilly, we are told, was not.

The Big Wind

Michael Kilkelly tells a story relating to Andy Melia's trade. He was a popular local slater. There is a record of him being paid £2 for repairs to the roof of the court house in 1842. However, Kilkelly's story relates to 'the Night of the Big Wind' in 1839, when Andy was employed to repair damages to the roof of Thomastown House and its outbuildings.

The steward of the estate conveyed Andy in his trap to the house and pointed out to him the various areas of damage which he was required to repair. Andy at once proceeded to his work. Whilst engaged in a turret, he was accosted by Tom Naughten's father, who was advanced in years and somewhat eccentric.

He asked Andy what he thought of the surrounding country-side as viewed from the turret. Andy answered that he was so enraptured at its magnificence that he found himself pausing in his work to admire it. Never had he viewed such a charming property and he had worked on Lord Castlemaine's property at Moydrum Castle, John Longworth's at Glynwood, Augustus Temple and others.

Just then the luncheon bell rang and Mr Naughten invited Andy to have a special drop of old whiskey with him. Andy declared that he found Athlone whiskey bad for his work. He was assured that this good old whiskey would have a different effect. Andy reluctantly consented and a decanter was produced. He swallowed a mouthful, closed his eyes and slowly savoured it; he agreed that it was far beyond any he had ever tasted. He was pressed to try another glass, which he 'reluctantly' accepted. He excused himself to go back to work but old Mr Naughten insisted and 'pressed' a third glass on Andy. Afterwards, recalling the story, Andy gloated at the way he had pulled Mr Naughten's leg by feigning ignorance.

In October 1859, Patrick Lennon was summonsed by Andy Melia for an assault which took place on the nineteenth of the month. The facts of the case as stated were that the complainant went to Melia's house to have an explanation of some language used which was unpalatable 'to him and his'. The defendant seized him by the neck and ran him out of his house. He was fined £1 and costs of 6s 6d, or a month's imprisonment, one third of the fine (if paid) to go to the plaintiff.

Athlone Man Fires the First Shot

In May 1898, the newspapers carried a report on the 'Athlone Man who opened the ball between Spain and America by firing the first shot'. The story concerned Gunner Patrick Melia, who was the son of James (Jim) Melia, a slater and plasterer, who left Athlone some forty years earlier and who, after an adventurous career in the American army, settled down to his trade in Jersey City. Patrick was the grandson of Andy Melia described in this account as a 'well remembered wag and local celebrity'.

Patrick fired the first shot against Spain and ended up being entitled to $460 as his share of the prize money gained by the capture of the ship *Bona Ventura*. The money, it was claimed, was 'but a trifling consideration' in comparison to the fame of the occasion.

The newspaper account recalled that 'old Andy', Patrick's grandfather, was known as 'Bracket Andy' because of a slight facial impression left by smallpox. 'Andy,' it said, 'was a sort of leader in every game among his class and from bladderman in the annual troupe of wren boys to the entertainer-in-chief of a rural wake he had no equal.' The account also states that another son of Andy's, also called Andy, had left Athlone twenty-eight years earlier and, after service in the British and American armies, joined the American navy.

It is remarkable that a century after Gunner Patrick Melia was celebrated in Athlone for having fired the first shot in the war against Spain and for his part in the capture of the *Bona Ventura*, his name is quite forgotten.

5

The Story of the Bells of St Mary's

The old square bell-tower adjoining St Mary's Church of Ireland in Church Street is one of the last vestiges of the church built by Oliver Lord St John Grandison in Athlone in 1622. The tower, with its barrel-vaulted ceiling at ground-floor level, has been added to (and subtracted from) over the intervening years. Twice in the eighteenth century substantial new additions were added to the tower, and in 1839, during the 'Big Wind', a wooden super-structure was dislodged from the top of the tower. Apart from its appeal as a relic of the earlier church, the tower is also interesting in its own right. Mrs Eliza Goldsmith, wife of Dean Goldsmith of Elphin (a cousin of the poet Oliver Goldsmith), is buried in this tower. She died in 1769 and the bell that tolled for Eliza was, most likely, the bell which was sounded by Godard de Ginkle to signal the final assault on the bridge of Athlone in 1691.

The bell of St Mary's was the subject of a rare pamphlet called 'The Story of our Bell', which was written by Revd John Swift Joly, rector and vicar of Athlone, based on a lecture which he delivered in Athlone on 11 January 1881. It was published in Dublin by George Herbert, 117 Grafton Street, in 1881. The following article is based largely on the content of that pamphlet.

St Mary's Church of Ireland in the 1950s.

A Description of the Bell

The bell has a legend on it, which reads as follows, 'This for St Mary's Chvch in Athlone 1683 T.C.' The text is in letters three quarters of an inch in height, which run around the bell between bands two inches from the shoulder. The text is interspersed with decorations, including *fleurs-de-lis* and bells. The bell itself is twenty-two and a quarter inches high to the shoulder; 25.5 inches to the top of the crown, which is nearly flat; about 8 inches in diameter; 48 inches in circumference at the shoulder, and 29.5 inches in diameter at the mouth. Revd Joly describes the sound of the bell as 'E natural' and notes that it is estimated to weigh over 6 cwt. It is cast without canons, and is attached to the stock by four bolts passing through holes in the crown.

Joly goes on to quote a report by Mr Richard Langrishe, an architect working with the Church of Ireland in the west of Ireland, then living in Athlone at Shamrock Lodge and late at Creggan. Langrishe states:

> A fracture to the middle of the sound-bow, shows the metal to be compact and good there, though the waist of the bell is somewhat honey-combed, owing, probably, to a deficiency of spare metal in the casting. It is well moulded, except the lip, which is ... too thin; consequently it has been much chipped round the edge, showing that it has been often laid on its mouth and carelessly handled.

The Tradition Regarding the Casting of the Bell

The tradition as handed down by Revd Joly is that the bell was cast in St Mary's churchyard and that the day of casting was observed as a 'high holiday'. We are told that no vehicle was allowed to pass through the street and that the townspeople came out and cast gold and silver coins and trinkets into the melting pot.

There was a tradition of casting (or recasting) bells in the churchyards of Ireland, the reason being that a church bell was cumbersome to move and was both weighty and fragile. We know of documented cases of bells being cast in the precincts of the cathedrals of both Kilkenny and Limerick. Revd Joly speculates that the prohibition of traffic:

> ... may have been rendered necessary by the close proximity of the narrow street [then considerably more narrow than at present having been widened by seven foot in the nineteenth century and by considerably more in the late 1950s], lest the vibration caused by the passing vehicle should disturb the mould or the setting of the metal.

'T.C.', the Bell Founder

Revd Joly was fortunate in having the scholarship of Richard Langrishe, architect and antiquarian, upon which to draw. Langrishe, a native of Kilkenny, had been involved in the relocation of a bell from the parish church of Dunmore to the steeple of St Mary's, Kilkenny. The bell was one of a pair cast in 1682 for the Duke of Ormond, the second being found in the campanile of the stables facing the gate of Kilkenny Castle. These bells, which are 'beautifully moulded', were cast on the lines of the Athlone bell, but were considerably smaller, and both had the initials 'T.C.' and the same *fleurs-de-lis* and bell ornamentation. The two great bell founders of that period were Roger Perdue and Covey & Associates. Richard Langrishe discovered an entry in the 'Acts of the Dean and Chapter of Christ Church, Dublin' from June 1686, when it was agreed to employ Tobias Covey to 'take down the great tenor bell of Xt Church, and cast it anew'.

Recast from the Plundered Bell(s) of Clonmacnoise

The tradition of the casting of the bell in the churchyard may have been the second coming for this bell. In other words, like the great tenor bell of Christ Church, it may have been recast in 1683 from an earlier bell or bells. Tradition is very strong in suggesting that the bells of St Mary's were originally from Clonmacnoise.

There is ample evidence in many sources about the bells of Clonmacnoise. In *Notes on Irish Architecture* by the Earl of Dunraven and Miss Margaret Stokes, passages are quoted from both Dr Petrie and from the *Annals of the Four Masters*, which would help corroborate this tradition:

> We have decisive evidence in the Annals of the Four Masters, to prove that this tower [O'Rorke's] of Clonmacnoise, if not the smaller one also, was appropriated to the use of a belfry, and known by the same name as originally, so late as the year 1552, when Clonmacnoise was plundered by the English garrison of Athlone – an event which the tradition of the place still preserves with all details, as if it had been only of recent occurrence. [p.34]

And:

> The final destruction of Clonmacnoise at the time of the Reformation, is thus described in the Annals of the Four Masters, 'AD 1552, Clonmacnoise was plundered and devastated by the Galls (English) of Athlone, and the large bells were taken from the 'Cloictheach' (bell house). There was not left, moreover, a bell small or large … which was not carried off.'

Joly goes on to reason that if the bells were carried off by the 'Galls of Athlone' then they may well have been transported to Athlone. Those who carried them off were 'champions of the reformed religion' and therefore 'we can have little hesitation in connecting them with the Protestant place of worship in the town'.

Revd Joly's original lecture was given, I'm sure, to an exclusively Protestant audience and Joly could not resist displaying his distaste for the Catholic Church. He revelled in the fact that the bell had been removed from Clonmacnoise by the English, as the following paragraph will reveal:

> Sometimes after a lengthened sequestration, property reverts to its rightful owners; and here is a remarkable instance. In the early days of Clonmacnoise, when it was the 'Retreat of the Sons of the Noble', when St Kieran founded the Abbey in the year 548, when it was the centre of learning and of opulence, and when our bell may have received its first birth and baptism, there was no such thing known as Roman Catholicism. The religion of Ireland was then essentially what Protestantism is now – religion according to the Word of God. Roman Catholicism came into Ireland, yea, into the world, at a very much later period, as an innovation, usurping the Establishments which belonged exclusively to a Bible Religion. Our bell, when carried by the Athlone Garrison to St Mary's Parish, was only restored to its primitive use to ring out the Grand Old Story that Jesus Christ is the way, the truth, and the life, and that no man cometh unto the Father but by Him.

Revd Joly goes on to speculate about where the bell was first erected, having been recast in the churchyard.

The Bell-Tower

The author tells us that he had taken it for granted that the position occupied by the bell in his day was the position in which it was originally erected. However, having read the old vestry books, he discovered that:

St Mary's façade and bell-tower, *c.* 1900.

... at the close of the last century [1790] an addition of about thirty feet was made to the steeple, for the express purpose of providing a belfry for Our Bell, for its better security. Until this addition was made ... the bell was someway connected with the steeple, probably upon the top, protected, perhaps from the weather by a canopy of wood. The steeple having being raised was surmounted by a wooden spire, thirty feet in height, and topped with a weathercock and gilded ball. This spire was blown down by the great storm of 1839, the massive and well-wrought iron vane part of which is at present in one of the lofts of the steeple.

According to Donal O'Brien in *Athlone, a Visitor's Guide*, 'the spire's weather vane was replaced on top of the belfry in 1945 following a restoration of the tower'.

Joly's Version of the War of the Kings

We know that the bell of St Mary's was sounded by Ginkle to signal the final assault on Athlone during the siege of 1691. Joly takes his account of the siege from Lord Macauley's *History of England*, but he prefaces his remarks with his own view of the Williamite and Jacobite Wars:

In its [the bell's] infancy came troublous times, and it was its lot to take part in the great wars of our country. A king arose [James] in whose eyes the glorious work of the Reformation was not merely a gross blunder, but a great sin as well. He sought to pull down the new constitution of England, and to re-enthrone Roman Catholicism. This was too much for England; she would not endure it; and she lifted up her hand and beckoned over to her help, a Prince [William] of great wisdom and ability, a religionist of true Protestant sentiment, a hero in the largest and every sense of the word; and, yielding to this sacred call, on Sunday, the 4th day of November, 1688, William, Prince of Orange, landed at Torbay, the Deliverer of these countries from the tyranny of a cruel bigot, and the thraldom of an intolerant religious system. A part of the role of this great man was the destruction of the power of James in Ireland; and, passing over such events as the Battle of the Boyne, we come to that which stands in immediate connection with the story of our bell – the Siege of Athlone.

He quotes at length from Macauley:

It was six o'clock. A peel from the steeple of the church gave the signal. Prince George of Hesse Darmstad and a brave soldier named Hamilton, whose services were afterwards rewarded with the title of Lord Boyne, descended first into the Shannon. Then the grenadiers lifted the Duke of Wurtemburg on their shoulders, and, with a great shout, plunged twenty abreast up to their cravats in water. The stream ran deep and strong; but in a few minutes the head of the column reached dry land.

The rest, as they say, is history.

The Pastoral Importance of the Bell

Having written about the history of the bell, Revd Joly then went on to highlight its pastoral importance to the parish of St Mary's. The bell was used in the ceremony of 'induction' of a new incumbent in the church, 'A beneficed clergyman of a neighbouring parish met the new incumbent at the church, and delivered into his hands the key of the door. The new incumbent tolled the bell, to announce to his parishioners that he had become their minister.'

Of course, the chief function of the bell was in calling the faithful to pray, but it also rang to mark baptisms, marriages and funerals. In looking at the registers, Joly speculates that the bell may have sounded for the baptism of one James Campell in 1769. The entry in the registry reads, 'James Campell, son of Dunkin and Juday Campell, born 22 of Disember, 1769, with tow of his fore teeith well growen, and was baptized by ye Revd Ellias Handcock, Cuaret of St Mary's, Athlone, 1769.' Joly adds his own comment, 'As this graphic pen [that of the parish clerk] has recorded no act of cannibalism, it may be inferred that this precocious youth shed those "tow" formidable "teeith" before he was "well grown".'

The bell was damaged in 1869, suffering a fracture from the lip to the middle of the sound bow. The damaged parts were deposited in the parish's 'iron safe' and the brilliance and tone of the bell were greatly diminished. Joly suggests that perhaps it should be recast by a 'modern day Tobias Covey' in the churchyard. He even suggests the legend the newly cast bell should carry, 'Carried off to Athlone from Clonmacnoise, AD 1552. Recast in St Mary's churchyard by Tobias Covey, AD 1683. Rang Ginkell's signal in the Siege of Athlone, AD 1691. Again recast in St Mary's churchyard by _____, AD _____.' Of course now it is most unlikely that anyone would ever be allowed to tamper with this historic artefact.

St Mary's has a second, smaller bell. In his guidebook *Athlone, the Shannon and Lough Ree*, published in 1897, Professor G.T. Stokes states, 'The other and smaller bell belonged formerly to the Tholsel or Market House, situated at the Leinster end of the present bridge.' The Tholsel was built in 1703 in the present Custume Place, facing down into Northgate Street. It was the centre of market activities, a place where election hustings took place, and where miscreants were put on public display in the stocks – exposed to the jeers and missiles of passersby. The Tholsel fell into disrepair and was dismantled in the 1830s. Had Professor Stokes not recorded the provenance of this second bell we might never have learned of its origins.

6

'Like the Devil
through Athlone'

My introduction to local history came when I was young and impressionable in the family home. Thinking back to the 1960s and '70s, I am constantly reminded of Billy English, who was a weekly visitor to our house. When he was writing an article or preparing a talk or lecture, or encouraging my own late father to write an article, he would call in to our house twice or three times over the weekend. Billy was always on a quest for knowledge and, though only ten at the time, I have a clear memory of the excitement surrounding the founding of the Old Athlone Society. It was then a society of 'youthful' enthusiasm; at the time my own father was forty-seven and Billy English a mere forty-three.

The Old Athlone Society has something for everyone. It was a family-oriented group and we had a family membership from the beginning. Even as children we felt very much involved. Volunteers were needed for various surveys: graveyards; recording inscriptions in stone around Athlone; collecting billheads and promotional material from local businesses; scouting for images of old Athlone. Once the museum was founded in 1967, on a rather *ad hoc* basis, volunteers were needed to write out museum labels, to sweep floors, and to help out with supervision (at that time many exhibits were just laid on open trestle tables).

One of my earliest assignments was to collect and type up poems about Athlone and its environs, and this modest effort has perhaps saved some gems of local poetry from oblivion. The poems ranged from the well-known 'A Ballad of Athlone', to ballads about the famous Athlone greyhound 'Lost Light', and the story of how 'Sidney held the Gates' during a famous water-rates controversy in Gentex. In terms of my introduction to the fascinating world of local history, I often think that it really was learning the easy way.

'Like the Devil through Athlone'

Only last week I received a query which was forwarded to me by Carmel Duffy, who manages the excellent www.athlone.ie website. Somebody had emailed from Wexford enquiring about the significance of an expression which contained the words 'like the devil through Athlone'. I was aware of the saying; the first time I heard it was from Billy English, well over thirty years ago.

Billy had it and had seen a quotation attributed to Rudyard Kipling, and so he was keen to find out more about it. He approached my predecessor in Athlone Library, the late Ernan Morris; we got as many of the works of Kipling as we could and Billy searched in vain for the quotation. A few months later, while leafing through some old copies of a magazine called *Notes and Queries*, published in April 1900, he came across a letter about the use of the expression during the recent Boer War. Today, of course, such research has become so much easier. I Googled the term, got access to *Notes and Queries* online, and was able to re-familiarise myself with the quotation.

Account Published in the *Daily Chronicle*

The correspondence in *Notes and Queries* started because of an account in the *Daily Chronicle* which read:

The Boers and the Dublin Fusiliers

Just before battle the Irish Brigade with the Boers sent a note to our Dublin Fusiliers saying that they would be glad to get the opportunity to wipe them off the face of the earth. The note was returned by the Dublins to say that they would walk through the Irish Brigade as the devil did through Athlone.

The querist stated that the account referred to the Battle of Tugela at Colenso (first attempt) and asked if any of their readers could 'furnish an explanation of the tradition of the devil walking through Athlone'. The Battle of Colenso was an engagement during the Second Boer War when the British, under General Sir Radvers Buller, made three attempts to end the Boer siege of Ladysmith. The military operation, which is generally known as the Relief of Ladysmith or the Battle of Tugela Heights, took place in February 1900.

Very soon, someone using the initials H.A.S. responded under the heading 'The Devil walking through Athlone'. He wrote:

I keep the above heading though it is enough to make any good Irishman shudder. The Devil never 'walked' through Athlone. He *went* through it, according to a modern version 'in standing jumps' but according to the vernacular speaking natives of the West coast, as I knew them thirty years ago it was 'in a lep [*sic*], a hop and a standing jump'. The phrase was always used of a hurling match or a faction fight, in which one side, or one particular hero of it, had 'gone through' the opposing lines with rapidity and completeness, hence its use as a threat by an Irish regiment to the so called Irish Brigade in South Africa recently.

Someone else put forward the theory that it referred to the Devil clearing everything before him and that it clearly referred to the cruelty of Oliver Cromwell in Athlone. This theory was quickly dismissed when it was pointed out that there was no record of Cromwell ever having visited Athlone.

Rudyard Kipling

In Rudyard Kipling's *Soldiers Three*, there is a story of how Mulvany prevented the elopement of his colonel's daughter, 'Mother av Hivin! But I made that horse walk, an' we came into the Colonel's compound as the Divil went through Athlone – in standing leps. There was no one there except the servints, an' I wint round to the back and found the girl's ayah.' This book was first published by A.H. Wheeler in Allahabad in 1888.

A further quotation from Kipling was recorded by Andrew Barton 'Banjo' Paterson (1864-1941) in his book *Happy Dispatches*, first published in Sydney in 1935:

> I must buy a house in Australia some day. I've a house here, and in New York and in Capetown but I'd like to live in Australia for a while. I've been there, but I only went through it like the devil went through Athlone, in standing jumps. You can't learn anything about a country that way. You have to live there and then you can get things right. You people in Australia haven't grown up yet. You think the Melbourne Cup is the most important thing in the world.

The phrase is also to be found in the writings of Sommerville and Ross.

I still haven't discovered where the saying originated, or exactly what it means, but suffice it to say that it was in wide use in late Victorian times and most likely had its origins in some story which circulated through military channels. There were soldiers who were either recruited in Athlone or who served in Athlone and who later saw service during the Crimean and Boer Wars. Perhaps this was a phrase which was once in common currency in Athlone; the 'devil' may have been the personification of cholera or another dreaded disease – perhaps ophthalmia, which was rampant in Athlone in the mid-nineteenth century.

7

The Royal Hotel

The recent announcement of the sale of the Royal Hoey Hotel heralds a new era in the life of this interesting site. Apart from the hotel itself, which has a history of hospitality stretching back over a couple of hundred years, the site also housed an old dispensary, a church for St Mary's parish (predecessors to those in St Mary's Place), and Athlone Printing Works.

In common with other Athlone hotels, the Royal Hotel evolved from being a nineteenth-century inn. The words 'inn' and 'hotel' are almost interchangeable. In bygone days, the word 'inn' was applied to a house which was open to the public for both lodging and the entertainment of the public. The inn frequently had its own stabling, thus providing accommodation for both man and beast. One such establishment in Athlone a century earlier was Luscomb's Hotel, which the local historian James Hill believed occupied the same site as the present-day Royal Hotel.

By 1729, 'Innholder' James Galvin was the lessee of this plot, but it seems likely that the original builder of the house was a member of the Kelly family. Three generations of Kellys lived here in the eighteenth century; one of them, James Kelly, was a 'linen manufacturer'. In 1786, James Kelly moved to Garden Vale and his son Thomas moved into Mardyke Street. It was Thomas Kelly who opened the Sun Hotel here in 1803, according to an advertisement in the *Athlone Herald* in July of that year, 'Thomas Kelly of Athlone most respectfully begs leave to acquaint the Nobility,

The Royal Hotel, note the Royalette Ballroom to the left.

Gentry and his Friends that he has opened a large and extensive Hotel on a plan and scale hitherto unknown in the town.' He promised that it would be his constant study and care to have his vaults well stocked with the best wines, his larder well supplied, his beds well aired, choice stabling, carriages with careful drivers and good coach houses. Had these standards been upheld by all his successors we would have had a very worthy inn, but sadly, during the nineteenth century, the standards declined. In 1832, Isaac Weld wrote, 'On the Leinster side stand the only two houses which deserve the name of Inns, and these are very indifferent although the business is considerable.'

Kelly was succeeded by Arthur Broom Garty and then by Robert Haire in the 1830s. Arthur Garty was the son of John Garty, who had held a grocer's shop in Mardyke Street in 1766. In Cromwell's *Tour Through Ireland* (published 1820) there is a view of Mardyke Street in which the hotel appears. There is a sign board swinging from the facade which depicts a sun and the name Garty. This was the old Sun Inn. The proprietor, Arthur Garty died in 1834.

Haire's Hotel

Robert Haire, a publican from Dublingate Street, seems to have become involved in the running of the Sun Inn following Garty's death. Haire was already involved as an agent for the mail-coach service, so the stabling and coach houses would have been of considerable interest to him. A notice in the *Westmeath Independent* in 1834 advised the public that Robert was 'about to start a two horse car to Roscommon from Haire's Hotel'. Robert Haire died in 1840. Perhaps because of ill health, or simply a desire to retire, Haire had advertised the Sun Inn to let in the *Athlone Sentinel* in July 1839:

> To be let for such terms as may be agreed upon that large and commodious house, shop, and concern known as The Sun Inn. From its situation, being in the best street in Athlone, from the extent of its concerns, and being long established as a Hotel, it is worthy to the attention of Capitalists. Application to be made (if by letter, post-paid) to Denis B. Kelly. Esq., Johnstown, Athlone or to Thomas McBride Esq., 17 Westmoreland Street, Dublin.

During Robert Haire's time, the hotel enjoyed a reputation as a place of entertainment. Many shows and performances were held there. It was in 'Haire's Great Room' that the American Negro tragedian Mr Ira Aldridge, known as 'The African Roscius', had performed from his Shakespearean repertoire during his visit to Athlone in 1838. This was just five years after he had played Othello at Covent Garden, and we know that he performed an excerpt from Othello here also.

The Royal Hotel

Robert was succeeded by his son, also Robert, but he died young in 1842 and the business passed to his brother William. It was

William who renamed it the Royal Hotel. The earliest recorded mention of the name is 1848. A March 1863 newspaper account of the 'illuminations' in Athlone states, 'Haire's Hotel exhibited the only attempt at illumination by gaslight, a Prince-of-Wales Plume in flaming jets lighted up the end of the street.' One wonders if, when his competitor Patrick Bergin decided to rename his town-centre inn the 'Prince of Wales Hotel', he made a bid to Haire for the gas sign.

Traveller Julius Rodenberg, who published an account of his tour in Ireland, entitled *Pilgrimage through Ireland*, in London in 1860, gives a grim account of his experiences in the hotel. He had travelled to Athlone by a Shannon Steamer from Killaloe:

> Now our voyage was at an end, we stopped at a broad weir, over which the Shannon falls like a cascade. Slightly elevated over it, and with a fresh breeze from the water blowing through its streets, is Athlone. I went up the landing steps to the dam where a carriage from the 'Royal Hotel' was waiting. I certainly saw in Ireland all sorts of vehicles, such as I had no idea of before, but one like that belonging to the 'Royal Hotel' of Athlone never crossed my vision before or after. It was a coffin nailed upon two wheels. Not an actual coffin, if I wish to adhere to the truth, but an edifice which looked like nothing on earth as much as a coffin. It was lined inside with black, and rags like widows weeds hung down from the seats. The coffin had no window, but a door, and through the door poured, in addition to a certain amount of light, more wind than a man, whether he be dead or alive, can stand. I had no notion of the route the coffin conveyed me; only at times, through a dizzy feeling that came over me, and the increased draught through the door, I noticed that I was turning a corner.

Rodenberg goes on to relate the apprehension which he experienced on entering the Royal Hotel, 'The Hotel-keeper's shirt hung out, and "Boots" yelled because the waiter hit him over

The Royal Hotel, *c.* 1940. (Courtesy of Ms Katie McCay Duffy)

the head with a gun which had somehow come astray amid my luggage. The coffee room looked as if it had not been swept or cleaned since the creation'. Despite his hunger and thirst he took himself in search of alternative accommodation, sadly his experience in the Prince of Wales Hotel was not much better – here he 'ate bread and cheese, drank sour beer …'

William Haire married Elizabeth Lynch in 1843. She lived to be a great age and managed the hotel at two different periods; firstly when her son was a minor and later, following the death of her son in 1899. A contemporary letter to the paper towards the end of the nineteenth century, and signed simply

'A Rambler', sang the praises of Mrs Haire, 'Put up at the Royal for the Evening and right royally was I served an excellent dinner – Shannon salmon, Galway lobster – the hostess, Mrs Haire, a friendly and good natured lady'.

The Twentieth Century

The modern history of the hotel is summarised by the late Frank Egan in his book *Bridging the Gap: Athlone's Golden Mile, 1920-1980*:

In the early 1920s, this was Claxton's Hotel, doing a very popular middle-class town and country trade. It had huge stabling yards, and the proprietor Dick Claxton was also an undertaker when horse-drawn hearses were the norm. After Dick's death in the late '20s, his widow carried on the hotel but closed the undertaking business. In later years, after her death, the hotel was run by the Hoey family who in the late 1940s took over two adjoining shops, Claffey's and Egan's, and started a huge reconstruction scheme. By the time James Hoey died in 1973, he and his wife, Mary, had built up one of the finest provincial hotels in Ireland. Under Mrs Hoey's personal supervision, assisted by her genial manageress, Miss Downes, it is a first-class hotel catering for social and commercial interests.

In the twenty years since Frank Egan wrote this account, Mrs Mary Hoey continued to run the hotel. The Royal Hoey Hotel has been the venue for all sorts of meetings, conferences and courses. Clubs and societies have met there on a regular basis and the hotel has been an integral part of the social and cultural life of the town. In wishing Mrs Hoey great happiness in her retirement, one can only hope that this hotel or its modern successor will serve the growing needs of the population of Athlone over the next 200 years as well as the Royal Hotel has served its needs in the past.

8

The Story of Admiral Sir Ross Donnelly

I was always intrigued by a paragraph which I first read in the Strean Manuscript, a source which was given to Athlone Library with the Burgess Papers by their custodian, the late Jack Simmons, photographer, Northgate Street, in 1971. The Strean Manuscript is a rather quaint document written by Mrs Emily Dunne (*née* Mangin) in 1869 for her cousin Archdeacon Henry Strean of Delgany, County Wicklow. Mrs Dunne was brought up in St Peter's Glebe by her aunt Mrs Strean and in this manuscript she records her impressions of life in the Glebe, together with her memories of individual family members, etc. The paragraph in question reads:

When speaking of our dear old grand aunt, Mrs Mecham, I should have mentioned the history of a nephew of her landlady old Mrs Donnelly, a vulgar but good natured woman of very low connections in Athlone. She had a nephew, Ross Donnelly, a small boy who was 'boots' at the little old Inn of the 'Three Blacks' in the Main Street. This boy, Ross, became a cabin boy on board some vessel, and by degrees, through good conduct and natural ability rose to be a commander, then a port captain, and finally an Admiral!!! He also got a knighthood and became Sir Ross Donnelly. His eldest daughter married Lord Dudley [*sic*]; his youngest daughter, Anne, kept house for her father in Harley Street. We knew her well for years after her father's death.

Dr Burgess added his own notes to the Strean Manuscript, and one related to the above paragraph:

> Not quite as LOW as Mrs Dunne imagined. Francis Donnelly, apothecary, lived at No 9 Castle Street, and was most probably the father of Ross. The Donnellys had some connection with the 'Three Blackamoor Heads'. Ross Donnelly was born *c.*1761 'son of Dr Donnelly', see D.N.B., where an account is given of his career in the Royal Navy from 1780. K.C.B. 1837, Admiral 1838, died 30 September 1840. His eldest daughter, Anne Jane, married in 1816, George John 20th Lord Audley.

The Evidence of History

In the eighteenth century, it was common for the local apothecary to be referred to as 'Doctor', and this was most likely the case with Francis Donnelly, who seems to have been an apothecary in Athlone. The earliest reference to a Francis Donnelly was when he witnessed a deed in Athlone in 1715; the following year he was a pew owner in St Mary's Church of Ireland. It is not clear, from surviving records, whether he was the same Francis Donnelly who was described as an apothecary in a lease of No.9 Castle Street in 1744 – this was most likely the father of Ross Donnelly, who was born in Athlone around 1761. Sadly the lack of surviving records from St Peter's Church of Ireland means that we will never be able to pinpoint the birth and parentage of Ross Donnelly. If he ever served as 'Boots' in the Three Blacks it was as a very young man, since we know that he entered the navy early in the American War. His first posting was under Vice-Admiral Arbuthnot on the coast of North America. He was present at the capture of Charlestown, South Carolina in May 1870 and as a result of his service he was promoted to the rank of Lieutenant to serve on the sloop *Morning Star* in 1781. Two years later, after the Treaty of Versailles, he left to join the East India Company, but ten years later he returned to the navy.

In 1793, he was appointed first lieutenant of HMS *Montagu*, described as a 'third rate ship of the navy line' which was a seventy-four-gun vessel. He commanded the ship the following year, after the death of her captain, James Montagu, during what was known as 'the Glorious First of June' – the first and largest fleet action of the naval conflict between the Great Britain and France during the French Revolutionary Wars. Both Lord Howe, the distinguished naval commander, and Lord Bridport seemed very pleased by the conduct of the fleet and Donnelly expected to be decorated for his service. Instead, like the other first lieutenants involved, he was raised to the rank of commander in July that year.

Service under Nelson

In June 1795, Donnelly attained the rank of captain and was appointed to HMS *Pegasus*, a twenty-eight-gun frigate, in the North Sea, where he served with Admiral Duncan, the victor of the Battle of Camperdown. From *Pegasus* he moved to HMS *Maidstone* and in 1801 he helped rescue a convoy of 120 merchant ships from Oporto and was handsomely rewarded by the merchants of that city. Late in 1801, he served on HMS *Narcissus*, a thirty-two-gun fifth-rate ship which he commanded for the next three years in the Mediterranean as part of Nelson's fleet.

It seems that Nelson held Ross Donnelly in very high regard. When one of his own relations joined the navy, he confidently put him under Donnelly's care, as did he with other young men. To the father of one of these young sailors Nelson wrote, 'Your son cannot be anywhere so well placed as with Donnelly.'

To South America

The career of Ross Donnelly was an illustrious one. In 1805, while still aboard HMS *Narcissus*, he accompanied Sir Home Riggs Popham on his travels, firstly to the Cape of Good Hope and later when he led the attempt to promote a rising in Buenos Aires. (The Spanish colonists, though discontented, were not willing to accept British rule.)

When he returned to England he discovered that he was in great favour, having been mentioned in dispatches by Popham and others, and he was then appointed to HMS *Ardent*. The *Ardent* was a sixty-four-gun, third-rate ship of the line. She was originally designed for the East India Company but was purchased by the navy after the outbreak of the French Revolutionary War. Aboard *Ardent*, he returned to the River Plate, where he commanded a convoy of transports. He commanded the naval forces at the capture of Montevideo and earned great respect for his handling of matters. In 1808, he was appointed to HMS *Invincible*, a new seventy-four-gun ship which was launched in Woolwich that year. He served off Cadiz in Spain and afterwards at Toulon.

An Honourable Retirement

In 1810, due to failing eyesight, Ross Donnelly resigned his command. However, within two years he was sufficiently recovered to seek a new posting. Once again, he was given command of a new vessel, this time the HMS *Devonshire*, a seventy-four-gun ship which was built at Deptford, launched in September 1812 and which he fitted out. With peace, there was no need for *Devonshire* to put to sea and so Donnelly's career at sea came to an end. He was appointed rear-admiral in 1814, vice-admiral in 1825 and admiral in 1838. While vice-admiral he was made KCB (military division) in February 1837 and invested on 17 March that year. He died on 30 September 1840.

In the South West region of Australia there is a place called Donnelly River. Today it is a mere holiday village, but it was once a thriving town which was officially called Wheatley but generally known as Donnelly River. The town adopted the name of the small river which flows through it and on into the Southern Ocean. The Donnelly River itself was named by Governor James Stirling after Admiral Sir Ross Donnelly, who was apparently a friend of his wife's family.

Sadly, only a handful of people in Athlone have ever heard of Ross Donnelly, and yet in far-off Australia he is commemorated by both a settlement and a river named in his honour.

9

John Rafter the Writing Master

One of the high points of providing a weekly column to the *Westmeath Independent* over the years has been the feedback – thankfully mostly positive – that I have received from readers. Many people have contacted me and enabled me to complete the picture, as it were, by providing some vital piece of information. During the year, a good friend of this column, Mr Liam Gaffey, Castledaly, contacted me about John Rafter, writing master. He told me that behind his parent's pub, 'The High Chaparral' in Connolly Street, there was an outhouse which had once been the schoolhouse of a 'hedge school-master'. I now believe, as does Liam Gaffey, that this was where John Rafter had his little school.

In the early to mid-twentieth century, when local history was a very underdeveloped subject, the then editor of the *Westmeath Independent* had the foresight to encourage the study of local history by printing occasional articles by local scholars. A favourite contributor was Michael Kilkelly, a local businessman who was distinguished for many reasons, not least of which was his role in the nurturing of the talent of the young John McCormack.

Michael Kilkelly contributed occasional articles to this paper from as early as 1900, but his major contribution took the form of a series of articles about Athlone and its surroundings which appeared in the 1930s. These articles are invaluable to the local historian of today, as they capture and preserve many details about local people which otherwise would have been lost long ago. I have quoted from many of these articles over the years. One person of whom Michael Kilkelly painted a wonderful pen picture was John Rafter of Queen Street (now Connolly Street), who described himself as a 'writing master'.

Kilkelly's Description of Rafter

In Queen Street, over seventy years ago*, there lived a man named John Rafter, who kept a school for boys and girls. He was blind in one eye but he excelled in his hand-writing, which was like copperplate. His speech was high-toned and interlarded with big words. His services were very often availed of by applicants for situations and other benefits. The reading of these missives was heard by all the scholars with awe, as the language was of the most high-flown character.

Among the scholars was a boy named Thomas Finneran who had only one eye for seeing with, and, like Mr Rafter himself, this was the right one. It seemed co-incident, but in fact young Finneran became a splendid writer and even excelled his master in that accomplishment before he left school.

Many of the letters which Mr Rafter wrote for petitioners were addressed to the War Office on behalf of ex-servicemen, who were discharged after the Crimean War, and who desired an increase in their scanty pensions. He was successful on some occasions, as he deserved to be considering the stately and grandiloquent diction of his letters, which he never failed to read aloud for the edification of his scholars. His wife was very industrious; always knitting, sewing or darning, and she kept a lot of fowls in her yard, which did not cause her much outlay, as many of the scholar's lunches contributed a not inconsider-

* *It is important to realise that Kilkelly's article first appeared in the 1930s and thus when he refers to 'over seventy years ago' he was referring back to the period around 1860.*

able portion of their upkeep. Mrs Rafter used often to point to the different hens saying such a one was Celia Clarke's; another was Tommy Sproule's and so named them all for the different scholars who seemed pleased to be considered sponsors.

A Surviving Letter from Rafter

Some years ago, when I was researching the history of St Mary's parish, Athlone, I was delighted to find a surviving letter from John Rafter among the papers of Bishop McCabe in the Diocesan Archives for the Diocese of Ardagh and Clonmacnoise. The letter probably survived because it amused the recipient, or perhaps even merited being kept as an example of the calligrapher's art. The letter is written in an ornate copperplate style with beautifully formed letters embellished with flourishes which frequently commenced at the end of a word but finished up encircling the entire word. It is a fine example of the writing master's art, and the pleading tone of the letter gives us some example of the type of letter which he surely wrote on behalf of many an impoverished soldier, or perhaps on behalf of a local scholar who wanted to secure a position as a clerk or a postman:

My Lord,
The Almighty God whose throne is in heaven's centre, whose breath sustains worlds and to whom the most secret thoughts of our hearts are known, sees and knows my unfeigned gratitude for your Lordship's goodness in sending me a P.O. for 10/- when I was getting up a subscription that I might send my daughter to America. This I have done on the 8th May last. As my health was impaired I bowed a submissive obedience it been [*sic*] God's holy doing. The Holy Spirit dictated to me and I addressed His Holiness the Pope and He, God be thanked, sent me £4 in these words. 'By order of Cardinal Antonelli, in reply to Mr John Rafter's letter to the Pope, Cardinal Cullen sends

him the enclosed £4.' This holy reply I retain, and at death the words contained therein, shall be engraven on my heart.

My Lord, Before Him to whom the secrets of futility are open, I sorrowfully confess that I was induced to go to England (the polluted of God's beauteous creation) to try and make off [*sic*] a living for my children. I could have got two of them, females, into a factory but when I saw, O! it horrifies me to mention it, the abandoned characters who were in attendance there, I hastened back to the Island of Saints, the hearts of whom therein are as pure as our religion is sacred, and such was my poverty on arrival, as not to be able to get my children's dinner until Revd Fr Monahan sent me 2/-. I am now, thanks to God, in a neat house but, I lament to say that, on my return here, I pawned my feather bed in Dublin for 9/- and if I had it I would get 2/6 per week for one of my rooms, and in the name of that charity, of which your pious and impressive language bespeak your pure heart I call on you, my Lord, to lend me 10/- and before our Divine Redeemer I pledge myself to refund it at 1/- a week. With the uplifted hearts and hands of myself, my wife, and my four children, I pray that, the most choice blessings of heaven may attend your labours here, and may you be crowned with a crown of glory in the regions of light, and life eternal.

I am my Lord,
With sacred deference,
Your Lordship's Very Humble Servant,
John Rafter,
Writing Master,
Queen Street,
Athlone.　　5/8/[18]69

Sadly, we do not know whether this heartfelt plea for the 'loan of ten bob' had the desired result. However, as Rafter was living in the parish of St Peter's, we can assume that he was also sending a similar letter to the Bishop of Elphin!

10

Mr Gallagher the Ventriloquist

The back issues of our local newspapers provide a rich source of information about entertainment in Athlone during Victorian times. Sometimes troupes of travelling players or circuses arrived in the town, and put on a variety of shows and performances. At other times, individuals arrived and gave solo concerts, but one of the most colourful visitors was surely Patrick Gallagher, who was known to all and sundry, the length and breadth of Ireland, as 'Mr Gallagher'. In this article, based on materials researched by my late father, I will try to portray this character and give you, the modern reader, some insight into the type of entertainer who was popular in towns and villages throughout Ireland at that time.

From his debut in Dublin around 1827 until his death in 1863, 'Professor' or 'Mr Gallagher' the ventriloquist was one of the best-loved Irishmen both on and off the stage. Quite apart from his work on the stage, he was a noted practical joker, who loved to amuse onlookers by causing harmless embarrassment to others. A native of Chapilizod in Dublin, P.F. Gallagher was educated for the Church, but before he took Holy Orders he realised that his true vocation lay in the field of entertainment.

Gallagher in Mullingar

In March 1828, Mr Gallagher appeared in the Market House, Mullingar, by kind permission of Mr John Charles Lyons (Lyons is best known as a printer and publisher; he lived at Lediston outside Mullingar, and compiled and printed a book called *The Grand Juries of Westmeath*). Gallagher performed his show entitled *The Adventures of Richard or Family Perplexities*, with front seats costing 3s and back seats 1s 6d. He played to a good attendance on the first night and a crowded hall on the second night. So popular was his show that he returned in July for a repeat performance while *en route* to Longford, Boyle and Sligo.

In December 1833, Gallagher was back in Mullingar for a full week. The show, an updated version of his earlier piece, was *The Adventures of Richard the Ventriloquist or The Biter Bit*. In this two-act show Gallagher played no fewer than twelve different characters. The public were advised that 'A band will be in attendance. NB There will be fires kept in the room.'

Visit to Athlone

The *Athlone Sentinel* of 5 December 1834 carried the story 'Ventriloquist Postponement', in which Mr Gallagher announced to the 'nobility, gentry and inhabitants of Athlone and its vicinity that in consequence of objections raised against the Amateur Theatre as a place for his performance Major General Sir John Buchan has very kindly honoured him with the use of a spacious room in the Barrack'.

Gallagher was to perform his celebrated entertainment *The Biter Bit*, and the Major General, we are told, had ordered that free access (to the barracks) be given to 'the respectable portion of the inhabitants of the town'. Major Farquharson had also kindly allowed the attendance of the band.

A local newspaper review was high in its praise of Gallagher and noted that, 'The house on Monday night attended by all the rank, fashion and beauty of the town was crowded to excess.'

Those who were involved in running the Amateur Theatre in Athlone were furious at the manner in which his handbills claimed that they had objected to his use of their hall. They clarified the matter through the columns of the local press. He had in fact been given the use of the hall, but when he tried to remove property belonging to a local group he was challenged and so he decided to give back the keys and find an alternative venue.

Return Visits

The celebrated Mr Gallagher returned in 1839 to the Barrack Theatre in Athlone and in 1845 he appeared in 'The Old Theatre in Scotch Parade' opposite the Leinster chapel. In 1848, he was back to appear in the Temperance Hall in Queen Street, as well as a further show in the barracks. When he came to play in the Pavilion of Rourke's Hotel in 1856, he chose to stage his show called *The Bubble Family*.

The *Westmeath Independent* of 14 June 1856 carried the following story:

We have so often spoken of this gentleman's humorous powers that it is unnecessary to dwell on this now; instead we wish to quote from *The Lamp of '52* where an account of his amusing pranks was published ...

'In the market place of the ancient city of Cashel in the County of Tipperary, while walking one day with the late, most respected, Catholic Dean Ryan of that city, they came to the place where turf was exhibited for sale. Standing in a circle were about one hundred asses loaded with the fuel. Both the Dean and Gallagher stopped for a moment, when a brave athletic fellow stepped forward and said, "Maybe yer hounour I'd want as good a creel of black turf as ever burned on a hearth undher a pot o' lumpers."

"Wait till I see it – what's your name?" asked Gallagher.

"My name is Tim Daly yer honour," replied the poor fellow. Gallagher went near the ass in order to look at the turf when all of a sudden the donkey began to sing in a low plaintiff tone to a beautiful Irish Air ...

"Ah now, Mr Daly, I ask you gaily–"

"What's that," gasped Tim as he stepped back, while the ass continued ...

"Won't you raise my wages, from thirty shillings to one pound ten?"

All was amazement and confusion for a moment and even the good Dean, who was in on the secret, could hardly refrain from laughing outright. The ass continued, not to sing but to talk after the following fashion, "Ah, thin, Tim Daly, isn't it a burnin' shame for you to be tryin' to pass off this auld creel of turf on the gintleman for dry when you know in your sowl its as wet as dung."

"The Lord save us," says a woman, "but the ass is tawkin' so it is" and she took to her heels followed by several others, as fast as their legs could carry them.

Tim stood, like Tam O'Shanter's mare, "right sor astonished" and couldn't tell what to make of it, when the ass went on to say, "Well Tim Daly you're the biggest rogue in Tipperary so you are!" Tim couldn't stand this and he gave the animal such a clout of a wattle which he held in his hand that it fairly lifted the donkey off the ground. In order to avoid a repetition of such another the beast scampered off as hard as he could, followed by all the rest. The line was broken and men, women and children, asses and creels of turf were conglomerated together on the market place of Cashel in less than no time! Such a scene was never before witnessed in the ancient city and I'm sure will never again be seen there.

Gallagher returned to Athlone in 1860 and again in 1862. It was therefore with great regret that the people of Athlone read of his death in April 1863 at the age of sixty-three. He was a great supporter of local charities and never missed the opportunity to do a benefit performance for the poor. He died, we are told, 'at peace with God and with all mankind' and he had certainly managed to bring more than a little levity into Irish life during his long stage career.

11

Custume Barracks Explosion, 1925

My good friend Jimmy O'Connor of Goldsmith Terrace tells me that as a young boy he remembers being at school in the Marist Brothers when an explosion rocked the building. It was a Monday afternoon, and the explosion caused the large world maps to fall off the wall. Later that day, they were to learn the facts of the explosion in Custume Barracks, in which three men and a horse were killed. Mr O'Connor remembers one of the dead, a

British Troops leaving Custume Barracks.

Mr Kearney, and indeed to this day could give a good description of both Mr Kearney and his horse.

The Victims

The dead included two army privates and a local carter. Neither of the privates were natives of Athlone. One private, Daniel Tighe, was a native of Rathowen, County Westmeath, and the other, Private Joseph Hoey, was a native of Tullamore. Locally, there was widespread sympathy for the third victim, a popular local carter, Mr James Kearney (aged forty) who lived in Queen Street, Athlone. Mr Kearney was a hard-working civilian employed in the barracks but was a well-known figure around town with his horse and dray. A fourth person had a miraculous escape; he was local football hero Private J.J. Dykes, who had been part of the famous Athlone Town football team which had been victorious in the Free State Cup Final in 1924. Dykes, who was working on the roof of the shed in which the explosion occurred, was hurled through the air for a distance of thirty yards. His injuries, though not life threatening, put pay to his hopes of a soccer career. Only the previous weekend he had been approached by a representative of Aston Villa and invited to join that club.

The Tragic Stories of the Dead

According to a contemporary account of the tragedy published in the *Westmeath Independent* of Saturday 4 April 1925:

Pathetic circumstances surround the deaths of the victims. Private Tighe was due to leave for Ballinasloe, but the lorry in which he was to travel was delayed in starting and he had decided to help in the clearing of the shed. Private Hoey had been away for the week-end in Tullamore visiting a sick child,

Accommodation Road. The Barracks is on the left.

and had arrived in the barracks but a short time previous to the disaster. He was not yet dead when the announcement of his child's death reached Athlone.

Sergeant-Major Reidlinger, who accompanied the three victims to the yard in which the incident occurred, had turned back into the barrack square proper less than a minute before the explosion.

The Land Mine

The cause of the explosion was a homemade landmine which had lain in the barracks unnoticed since 1922. The landmine had apparently been removed from the old workhouse to the barracks but was deemed to be harmless. It seems that it had been recovered following an unsuccessful attempt to derail a train in south Westmeath.

Prior to the explosion, it had been noticed that one of the ends (or caps) of the homemade bomb had become loose.

It is thought that Mr Kearney, in an idle moment, may have been trying to unscrew it when the explosion occurred. Both Kearney and Tighe took the brunt of the explosion and were killed instantly – so great was the impact that neither body could be fully recovered. Mr Hoey suffered severe head injuries but survived for five hours.

J.J. Dykes was putting felt roofing on the shed when the mine exploded. 'All I know of the explosion,' he declared, 'is that I suddenly found myself on the ground a good distance from where I had been working. I thought my legs had been blown off, and stood up to see that it was not really the case.'

There were no eyewitnesses to the actual explosion. The shed was at a corner of the barracks, alongside Grace Road.

Windows Broken

Commadant Whelan, who was in his office about fifty yards away (the glass in the windows of the office was broken in the explosion), rushed out to find that the whole front of the shed was gone, nearly half the roof blown away, and timber, iron, felting and all sorts of other material strewn about the yard. Dykes, whom he had seen working but a short time before on the roof, was lying on the ground almost thirty yards away.

Almost immediately help was forthcoming from every part of the barracks, officers and men realising, from the violence of the explosion, that a disaster had occurred. The noise, in fact, was so great that it was heard a considerable distance outside Athlone. Making their way through the wreckage to where the shed had stood, the military were horrified to see the maimed and bleeding bodies. Private Hoey, who was still breathing, was hurried off to the hospital, but it was soon realised that his case was hopeless.

Mr Kearney left a widow and four children, and Private Hoey a widow and three children, while Private Tighe was unmarried.

The Inquest: Opened and Adjourned

The day after the explosion, the coroner, Mr Peadar Melinn, opened an inquest into the tragic deaths of three young men. Superintendent Hunt watched the proceedings on behalf of the Civic Guards and Comdt King BL represented the military authorities.

The following were sworn on the jury: Messrs Owen Dolan (foreman); James Grealy; Martin Murray; Denis O'Halloran; Bernard Fitzpatrick; John Lennon; James Kenny; Thomas O'Brien; James Connaughton; Edward Butler; John Grenham; Richard Jones; Joseph O'Meara, and Patrick J. Lennon.

The coroner explained that only formal evidence of identification could be dealt with that day as he would have to give notice to the authorities in Dublin so that an inspector could attend.

The jury then viewed the remains.

Commadant Whelan, Custume Barracks, gave evidence of identification of the bodies of Privates Hoey and Tighe, both of whom were attached to the National Army Headquarters, Athlone. Edward Kearney, his brother, identified the remains of James Kearney. The inquest was then adjourned for a week.

The coroner said he wished to convey his heartfelt sympathy to the relatives of the deceased in their very sad bereavement. It was a terrible occurrence, three men blown to pieces, without a moment's warning.

Funerals of the Victims

At two o'clock on Tuesday, the remains of Private Daniel Tighe were removed for interment to his native place, Rathowen, County Westmeath. The coffin, which was draped with the tricolour, was placed in a lorry and escorted from Custume Barracks as far as the post office, where a firing party was dispatched to accompany his remains to Rathowen.

The remains of Private Joseph Hoey were conveyed by motor to Tullamore, his native place, for interment. The coffin was similarly covered with the tricolour, and the same arrangements as regards escort were carried out.

The remains of Mr James Kearney were brought to St Peter's Church, Athlone, on the Tuesday evening and a Requiem High Mass was celebrated at eleven o'clock on the Wednesday morning. We are told that there was a large congregation present, which included nearly all the troops stationed in Custume Barracks, under the command of Captain Higgins. In accordance with the tradition of the time, the funeral took place at four o'clock that afternoon to Cornamagh Cemetery.

Military Negligence Alleged

'We find that the deaths of James Kearney, Joseph Hoey and Daniel Tighe were caused by the explosion of a landmine left in the store at Custume Barracks by the negligence of the military authorities.' This was the damning verdict of the coroner's jury, having heard the evidence.

Commadant Jas Ryan gave evidence that he was attached to the engineers at Custume Barracks. On 26 March he had sent a party to clear out the shed. They were working there until 30 March, the day of the explosion. The witness was present at eleven o'clock that morning and noticed something in the shed resembling a mine, and thought it had been a mine case. There was a plate on each side of it and both were very slack. The witness examined the thing and concluded that it was empty. The reason that this mine was overlooked was that the store was full of scrap and old stuff left there by the British.

Sergeant James Hardiman, National Army, deposed that he had been employed by the British in a civilian capacity years ago. During that time it was his duty to collect old scrap and put it in this store. The witness had a distinct recollection of the article described as a mine in March 1922. He took it into the store. The witness claimed that he never saw a road mine before that time, but it occurred to him that it was a road mine which was empty. It was left there for eighteen months and it was removed several times from one place to another in the shed.

One of the jurors, Mr Joseph O'Meara, put a question to the witness regarding how the mine came to be in the barracks in the first place. 'It was brought in and left outside the Engineer's Office … I did make enquiries at the time and I was told it was brought from the Workhouse, the IRA were there at that time.' To a further question, 'Is it customary to leave such things at the engineer's store?' Sergeant Hardiman replied, 'Yes, they were always left outside the door, and it was understood that I would remove them inside.'

In ascertaining his status, the jurors heard from Commadant Whelan that Mr Kearney was employed by the military authorities since 1922 and that his duties were to remove stuff to and from the stations and within the barracks itself. In reply to the question of whether Mr Kearney was a satisfactory employee, Commadant Whelan replied, 'He was a very fine fellow; one of the best workers in the barracks.'

Captain Thomas Henry deposed that he was Ordinance Officer since 1922 at Custume Barracks. He was in charge of all war material in the command. In July 1924, there was a lot of stuff in the barracks which was considered dangerous. An officer from GHQ came down to have it destroyed on 17 October. In response to a question from the foreman of the jury as to whether he was satisfied at the time that all the mines had been destroyed, Captain Henry replied that he was.

The jury recorded a verdict that the explosion was due to military negligence and recommended the relatives of the deceased to the consideration of the military authorities. The matter was subsequently raised in the Dáil in April 1925 by the local public representative Mr Sean Lyons TD.

12

Cockfighting: A Barbaric Pastime in Old Athlone

The ancient 'sport' of cockfighting was certainly practised in Athlone in the eighteenth and nineteenth centuries, but when it actually first found favour in the town remains a mystery. A deed of 1780 refers to 'a plot of ground commonly called the cockpit', which was owned by John Glass of Clonown and leased to Andrew Rutledge of Athlone. The plot, which was ninety-six feet in length and had a breadth of eighty-four feet, was located on a piece of open ground which then stood near the junction of Pudding Lane (Connolly Street) and High Street, on the Connaught side of Athlone. The old name for High Street was Cockpit Lane. In fact, the expanded streetscape to be seen in High Street today – between Fry Place and Bastion Street, in the vicinity of Quirke's Motor Factors – probably owes its shape to the presence of the cockpit in this area.

In cockfighting, two birds were set to attack each other until one of them was killed. In preparation for a fight, spurs of metal or bone were slipped over the natural spurs of the gamecock to make the fight more vicious. The 'sport' was a favourite with spectators, who often gambled large sums of money on the outcome of the deadly combat. In cockfights, given the volatile nature of the birds, the odds on one bird or the other fluctuate constantly and there are chances to gamble before, and indeed throughout, a fight.

It seems that cockpits appeared in Britain during the Tudor period, though cockfighting as a 'sport' goes back to the ancient world and was practised in India, China, Persia, and later in both Greece and Rome. Among the better-known fans of cockfighting was Henry VIII, who had a pit constructed at Whitehall Palace. For all his barbarism in other areas, it was Oliver Cromwell who moved to have the sport banned, but after the Restoration it gained a new popularity and pits were once again built in many towns and villages. It is possible that the cockpit in Athlone, given its relative proximity to the military barracks, was first established by soldiers (or officers) of the British garrison.

The Cockpit: Murder Most Fowl

While we do not know the dimensions or method of construction of the Athlone pit, they were usually about eighteen to twenty feet in diameter and surrounded by a barrier. Sometimes they were covered-in but others were left open. The floor was usually covered with turf or matting and the sides padded with hay. In Britain, a handful of cockpits have been preserved as national monuments. It would seem that the Athlone cockpit may have been rectangular in shape rather than the conventional round.

One of the earliest mentions I have found of the Athlone cockpit concerned a murder which was reported in the national newspapers on 17 December 1784. The account states:

> On Friday morning between the hours of two and three o'clock, Patrick Goff was murdered near the cockpit in Athlone ... Verdict of murder against Edward Meaghan who has absconded ... he was not found notwithstanding that Charles Stern, Sovereign of Athlone and a party pursued him on the same morning.

A Popular Pastime

Throughout the Stuart and Georgian era, cockfighting remained popular, attracting participants from every rank and class. It became big business, with birds bred specially and given names like racehorses. In fact, the sport was, in an odd sort of way, linked to horseracing through the involvement of the 12th Earl of Derby (1752-1834), the man after whom the famous Epsom 'Derby' is named. He was one of the most enthusiastic fighting-cock owners in Britain. It is said that at the height of his involvement, he possessed 3,000 fighting cocks, and, according to tradition, his first wife, Lady Elizabeth Hamilton, is said to have divorced him because of his insistence on holding cockfights in their drawing room. He later married Elizabeth Farren, a Drury Lane actress.

In Victorian times, the tide of opinion changed against cock-fighting and in 1849 an Act of Parliament was passed making it illegal to run public cockpits. Private cockfights were still permitted and of course, as we know, illegal cockfights are still not unknown in either Britain or Ireland today.

Cockfighting in Nineteenth-Century Athlone

In August 1824, the local newspaper reported on a cockfight between Fermanagh and Westmeath, which Westmeath were winning. Proceedings were then at an early stage, as the total encounter was to involve twenty-seven 'mains' and there were still nineteen to be fought. Westmeath had one bye and three mains, compared to Fermanagh's two byes and one main.

The mains (or matches) usually consisted of fights between an agreed number of birds, the majority of victories deciding the outcome of the main. There were two other versions of the sport which were even more frowned upon by those opposed to it: one was the 'battle royal', in which a number of birds were placed in the pit at the same time, with the last remaining bird becoming the victor, and the other was known as the 'Welsh main', in which eight pairs of cocks were matched, with the eight victors being again paired, then four, and finally the last surviving two were paired against each other.

In 1833, the local press covered another fight – this time a more parochial contest involving a 'main of cocks', as it was termed – being fought between the Leinster and Connaught boys. Of twenty-two cocks which fought, seventeen were killed and some of the other five were 'mangled and wounded'. The reporter stated that, 'A gentleman on the same day and in the space of one and a half hours saw eighteen tickets issued by a Pawn Office in the town on articles pledged for funds to be expended in this unworthy manner.'

Cockfighting Outlawed

By late Victorian times, whatever encounters did occur seemed to take place on the outskirts of the town, in quiet rural areas. Presumably the Act of 1849 had put pay to the Athlone cockpit, if indeed it had survived that long. From a report in a local newspaper, we learn that in June 1895 cockfighting took place on a Sunday morning at the Hill of Berries. Several 'tries' took place on the hill and we are told that 'the disgusting spectacle was witnessed by a considerable crowd'.

A further report in the local press, on 29 May 1897, reveals that a raid was made at 6 a.m. on a Sunday morning at a cockfight in Monksland. As a result of this raid, over a dozen summonses were issued. Those engaged in cockfighting included: Thomas Sherlock; Patrick Cooney; John Mills; John Lambert; Michael Lambert; Thomas Murray; Michael Crosbie, and Patrick Brien. The offences occurred on Sunday 16 May, when a group of fifteen to twenty were assembled at the 'pit'. John Mills was found with a bird under his arm which had been fitted with artificial spurs. Mills was fined £1 and the others, with the exception of Michael Lambert (owing to his youth), were fined 5s (or, in default, seven days in prison).

13

Fry Place: Athlone's Regency Terrace

Athlone is not noted for the quality of its architecture. The two railway station buildings, the castle and some of our churches are among the architectural highlights of the town. When you add to this a handful of fine shop fronts and doorways, you soon realise that, in comparison with other midland towns, we seem to have drawn the short straw. When judgement is passed on the late-twentieth-century additions to the urban infrastructure, some will pass with flying colours while other developments may leave

Fry Place in the early 1900s.

much to be desired. However, I for one feel that the refurbishment of Fry Place is one of the great success stories of modern Athlone; we have here preserved a fine Regency terrace, the only one of its type in the town.

Fry Place takes its name from a family who settled in Athlone in around 1738 and who took a lease of this site from Arthur St George in 1744. The St George family was one of two ruling families in Athlone, the other family being the Handcocks. For most of the eighteenth century, it was usual for a member of one or other family to hold the office of Sovereign of Athlone. The earliest member of the Fry family to settle in Athlone was Henry, son of John Fry of Edenderry. In 1738, he was described as 'a merchant' trading at 8 Church Street, Athlone. He was town bailiff in 1745 and a member of the Select Vestry in St Mary's Church of Ireland. By 1754, he was leasing one of the corn mills on the old bridge of Athlone. The Fry family continued to be prominently identified with life in Athlone until the 1830s.

No.1 Fry Place

Fry Place was built on the site of the Mansion House, an old building which was probably semi-fortified. The Ranelagh Estate map of 1784, reproduced in the Royal Irish Academy *Athlone Historic Towns Atlas*, records this as the site of the 'Mansion House'.

The first record to indicate the building of this fine Regency terrace is a deed of No.1 Fry Place, which is dated 1806. The numbering system on this terrace reads from right to left instead of the more usual left to right. According to this deed, it was occupied by Thomas Fallon and described as a 'dwelling house lately built by Henry Fry on the south side of Charles Kelly's house'. In 1808, it was occupied by Richard Holton and later by John Holton. The Holtons carried out a grocery business until around 1878, when the Hall sisters, Charlotte and Catherine (who were nieces of John Holton), took over the business. Charlotte was married to William Doyle, and on her death in 1900, the business was styled as 'W. Doyle & Co.'.

In 1922, the Irish National Foresters moved from King Street to Fry Place. A news item in the *Westmeath Independent* in the autumn of 1924 states that the 'fine new premises of the Irish National Foresters, Fry Place is undergoing a thorough renovation. Painters have been at work for the past fortnight. The frontage is being repaired and painted on most attractive and artistic lines.' And so it was until the mid-1980s, when the INF decided to restore the magnificent façade, which had fallen into disrepair. In October 1987, the late Nobel laureate Mr Sean MacBride performed the opening ceremony for the restored premises. Thus, the INF left a lasting legacy to the town of Athlone, before quietly closing the premises, which were to be taken over by Michael Cuddy, an accountant, on the upper floors, and Pavarotti's Restaurant on the ground floor.

The INF committee that tackled the fundraising and restoration of this fine façade was spearheaded by the late Mr Eamon Lacken. The other committee members were: Joe and John Blackweir; David and Paul Gibson; George and Ray Behan; Frank Kearney; James Duffy, and John Geoghegan

No.2 Fry Place

Next door, No.2 Fry Place was occupied by John Walker, a merchant, from 1808 to 1824. From around 1829 to 1840 it was the premises of John Doyle, grocer. Messrs Yates occupied the premises from 1862 into the early twentieth century. In November 1924, there was an application before the courts for a transfer of licence from Francis Yates to James Elliott. The Elliotts were a popular business family in Fry Place for almost fifty years. It is now the popular Angler's Rest lounge bar.

No.3 Fry Place

No.3, unlike the other three premises, was always a residential unit. In 1816, it was the dwelling house of John O'Beirne, a member of a well-known local distilling family, who remained there until 1845 (at least). By 1886 it was the residence of Dr Charles Joseph McCormack, a local general practitioner. McCormack was an early member of the Athlone Garrison Golf Club, situated on the Batteries, but his main claim to fame was that he was the father of Dr J.D. McCormack, the international golfer. Dr J.D. McCormack represented Ireland on twenty-four occasions between 1913 and 1937. His father, Dr C.J. McCormack retired in 1911 and was presented with a purse of sovereigns to mark his almost thirty years of service as a Medical Officer in the district.

In more recent times this was the residence of the Mulligan family.

No.4 Fry Place

No.4 was occupied by the Board of Ordnance in 1816, probably as a residence for a senior officer. By 1820, John Gaynor, a grocer, had opened his store there. In 1835 Gaynor was in partnership with Philip Hay. Hay died in 1861 and was succeeded by his nephew Thomas Phillips.

In January 1896, on the death of Mr Phillips, Mr O'Ferrall acquired this licensed premises and opened for business as publican and auctioneer. Mr O'Ferrall had acted as manager of Madden's in Church Street prior to this. Mr O'Ferrall died around 1950.

In January 1954, Joseph McFarland was granted the transfer of the six-day licence which was held in the name of Desmond O'Ferrall. By November of that year, there was an announcement that the public house, which had ceased to trade for over a year, was not now going to reopen. In December 1954, the premises reopened as a receiving depot for The Ivy Cleaners, with Mr Edward O'Brien as the local representative. Later, Mr McFarland, who had a furniture factory in Athlone since the late 1940s, opened the shop himself, selling new and second-hand furniture, televisions, radios and carpets. The remainder of the building was set in flats. In due course, the McFarlands transferred their entire business to Garden Vale and the premises continued to operate as rented accommodation.

The recent move of the award-winning Left Bank Bistro from Bastion Street to the ground floor of Nos 3 and 4 Fry Place brings a very welcome injection of life to these pivotal buildings. If I were to award my own personal accolade for a quality job of renovation in Athlone in this millennium year (and this year there was some stiff opposition), I would have no hesitation in awarding it to the developers of Nos 3 and 4 Fry Place.

14

Athlone Bicycle Club

Recently I was asked about a medal which was awarded by Athlone Bicycle Club in the 1890s, and it set me thinking about the great changes which have taken place in the bicycle industry over the years. Bicycles came into use in the middle of the nineteenth century. Experiments in the early nineteenth century in both France and Scotland had proved that the idea of a self-propelled bicycle was possible. In 1868, the first recorded bicycle race from Paris to Rouen was won by an Englishman named James Moore. He completed the eighty-three-mile course in just less than ten and a half hours. There was a field of almost 200 cyclists and Moore's bicycle had solid rubber tyres and weighed in at 160lbs.

A Daring Adventure by Tricycle

A contemporary newspaper account from 1886 gives us a wonderfully graphic description of a strange sight in Dublin:

On Monday afternoon when the crowd was thickest in the city a young lady of pretty face and pleasing figure did her shopping on a tricycle in Nassau Street. She was a young lady of quiet costume and modest lady-like demeanour. Here and there she pulled up close to the kerb-stone before the shop she wished to visit, alighted from her well trained and patient steed, passed into the shop and in a few moments emerged with the orthodox brown paper parcel which she deposited in a small and convenient little tray just behind the seat of the machine. She had quite a collection of such pieces on the tray when she finally stepped into her seat, as she might into a brougham, just there at the corner of Clare Street and turned her wheels towards home. Softly and easily she moved down the length of Nassau Street, wheeled gracefully into Grafton Street and slid away through the hurrying crowd of vehicles as noiselessly, as easily, and as safely as a bird upon the wing.

Athlone Bicycle Club

The sport of cycling was well established in Ireland by 1878, when it was administered by the Irish Cycling Association. Later, after the establishment of the GAA, cycling became part of GAA meetings. According to sports historian Dr Tom Hunt, the two different bodies had different constituencies; the Irish Cycling Association drew their members from urban areas, and these tended to be Unionists or moderate Nationalists, whereas the GAA opened the sport to the working classes, mostly from rural areas, and these tended to be strong Nationalists, so, inevitably, conflict arose between the two groups.

We do not know the precise date of the foundation of Athlone Bicycle Club but it seems most likely to have been 1892. In April of that year, the club held its first run to Birr. The cyclists left Athlone at 8.30 a.m. and reached Birr at noon. Having visited various attractions, including Lord Rosse's world-famous telescope at Birr Castle, they returned to Athlone in an even shorter time and the members expressed themselves well pleased with their day's outing. The next season began with a day trip to Longford on Easter Monday, when they visited Goldsmith's home in Auburn as well as the barracks and cathedral in Longford.

An Athlone cyclist – Gus Hynds, publican.

In the 1890s, there was a cycling boom when the penny-farthing was replaced by the 'safety bicycle', making bicycles cheaper and safer to use. The other great improvement around that time was the introduction of pneumatic tyres in 1888, and they gained popularity in the 1890s. Athlone cyclists were well served by M.H. Foy's store in Athlone. It claimed to have one of the largest and best-equipped workshops in Ireland, and was capable of carrying out all types of cycle repairs.

Second Annual Meeting in the Meadows

In August 1893, the Athlone Bicycle Club held its Second Annual Meeting. The day, we are told, 'was all that could be desired' and they met in the Queen's Meadows by permission of the colonel commanding the garrison. 'The country people flocked to the town, the fair sex in their brightest garb and it is estimated that when the first event took place there were some 5,000 people present.' Competitors had come from as far as Athy, Castlebar and Leitrim.

Among those present were: Mr Charles O'Donoghue, Ballinahown Court, High Sheriff for County Westmeath; Messrs Dogg, A.E. Johnston of Burgess; Thomas Chapman; R. Gladstone; T. Ahern; W.T. McElroy; J.P. Foy and W. Haire. The judges for the cycling were Messrs M. Kilkelly and J. Haddock. The telegraph steward was P. Ghent; lap stewards Sergeant McCarthy, J. McHugh, R. Moore and A. Ferry. The referee was R. Baile and the handicapper was Mr P.P. Sutton. M.J. O'Flynn and P. Duffy were the short call stewards.

M.H. 'Scorcher' Foy won the two-mile confined race, but the open races were all won by visiting cyclists. The captain of the Athlone club was Mr John McHugh, who worked in the furniture department of Thos Burgess & Sons. The Second Annual Meeting included a boy's race over 220 yards, which was won by M. Hogan from P.C. O'Flynn and William Egan.

Cycling Gains Popularity

At the AGM of Athlone Bicycle Club in March 1894, Mr Charles O'Donoghue was appointed as president of the club, with Mr P.B. Tracey and Mr James Conway as vice-presidents. The committee members included Messrs O'Flynn, Fry, Gladstone, Stitzel and Ghent, with Mr McHugh as captain.

The club held its first 'run' of the season to Moate on Good Friday, followed by a run to Banagher on Easter Sunday. When the club made a run to Ballinahowen Court in June, the party was entertained to afternoon tea by the club president.

The first road race of the 1894 season was in June. It was held over the Coolvuck course of ten miles. The following were the handicaps: Foy, scratch; Messrs Ferry, Jones, Heaton and Bacon four minutes, and Messrs Connell, Guinan and Connor six minutes. Sergeant Bacon won by six yards from Guinan, and Connor came in third.

A report in the local press in February 1895 tells us that when the entire expanse of Lough Ree was frozen over, skaters and cyclists could be seen on the lake. The ice was reported to be five inches thick.

In April 1895, various new members joined the ranks of Athlone Bicycle Club and these included: Mr James Lyster; Mr J. Gaynor, solicitor; Mr Charles E. Fair, solicitor; Dr McCormack, and Mr Michael Kilkelly.

An unfortunate accident marred the first run of the season that year. In April, twenty-three cyclists took to the road but a brake which was carrying spectators crashed at Cornamaddy. The horses apparently took off at a furious rate and broke their reins, leaving the driver helpless. Miss Conway and Miss Ghent jumped from the brake and were injured. The clothes of the latter were caught in the wheels and she was dragged some distance along the road. The horses were only brought to a standstill when they ran into a wall at Mr Kearney's place, and the entire party returned to town.

Apart from Athlone Bicycle Club, other clubs organised cycling events in Athlone in the 1890s. These included the YMCA and the Catholic Young Men's Society, and while members of both the local garrison and the RIC were involved in the Athlone Bicycle Club, the RIC also had its own designated club in Athlone and boasted a membership of forty.

15

T.P. O'Connor
& No. 10 Castle Street

It stands to reason that Castle Street is amongst the oldest streets in this town. We know that the earliest urban development in Athlone was in the vicinity of the castle during the Anglo-Norman period in the early thirteenth century. The castle itself, or at least parts thereof, date from the year 1210.

In a Ranelagh estate map of Athlone, drawn in 1784, this street was already known as Castle Street, while the present day Connolly Street was known as Pudding Lane. Other names in use as that time included 'Old Parade' for the present Market Square and Connaught Market Street for the present Main Street. There were houses built right around the perimeter of the castle, thus Castle Street had houses on both sides of the road (or, more correctly, narrow lane) which joined Old Parade with Connaught Market Street. The street which ran between the castle and the Shannon was known as Parade Street and it too had houses on both sides. The old Elizabethan bridge of Athlone, which had witnessed the Sieges of Athlone in 1690 and 1691, ran straight across from Bridge Street (on the east) to Connaught Market Street (on the west). The Shannon Navigation works of the 1840s and the building of the present town bridge were to alter the geography of these streets and to create the streetscape which we know today. Prior to this, the areas around Castle Street and the Old Parade were quiet backwaters adjacent to the military barracks.

The ruins of the birthplace of T.P. O'Connor, Castle Street, Athlone, *c.* 1927.

Thomas O'Connor: Billiard Saloon Keeper

It is uncertain when Thomas O'Connor arrived in Athlone, but we know that he was the son a Wexford man, another Thomas O'Connor, who he claimed was one of the first to take up arms at the memorable Battle of Vinegar Hill. Thomas himself was born sometime between 1811 and 1817 (depending on whether one takes his age from his headstone or his obituary). He was a small man, who was described as 'gentle yet very fearless'. He was a staunch Nationalist, a veteran of Fr Mathew's campaign, and, in his son's words, 'an exemplary Catholic' who was assaulted by the 'unfortunate women of the garrison, because supporting Keogh's opponent, he was supposed to be an enemy of religion'. The Keogh referred to was, of course, the notorious Judge Keogh (of Sadlier & Keogh fame), who stood for the Borough of Athlone.

According to tradition, before taking up his career as billiard saloon keeper, Thomas O'Connor was a failed tenant farmer in the parish of Drum. It seems that he was evicted after ten years of unsuccessful farming. An excellent article in *Drum and its Hinterland* (Drum Heritage Group, 1994) identifies Ardnagowna in connection with the O'Connor family and even suggests that T.P. may have been born there, but numerous references (including some of his own writings) would indicate that he himself believed he was born in Castle Street.

In August 1844, Mr Tracy, a billiard marker, charged two soldiers with assault. Tracy was employed by Mr O'Connor and claimed to have been assaulted by the two men, but it appeared that there may have been more 'horseplay' than assault and the case was settled out of court.

In 1848, at the time of the birth of his son Thomas Junior, who was to become better known to the world as 'T.P.', Thomas O'Connor was living in Castle Street. He later moved to Baylough, before returning once again to life in Castle Street. His property in Baylough consisted of a cottage and two acres of land – a site on which T.P. later built the Grove as a home for his parents. Thomas O'Connor Snr had married Teresa Power, the daughter of a Captain Power of the 88th foot regiment of the Connaught Rangers, then stationed in the military barracks in Athlone. According to the family tradition, Power had been an officer in the Duke of Wellington's army in Spain during the wars against Napoleon. Teresa was, we are told, a tall and dignified lady who was well spoken and the brains behind the family. Later, when T.P. became famous, she claimed that he had clearly inherited his intellect from her side of the family.

When T.P. was ten years old, his father was advertising himself as 'A Billiard Table Manufacturer'. His advertisement stated that Thomas O'Connor:

> ... having completed his arrangements for the manufacture of Billiard Tables on the newest and best principles is prepared to execute any order he may be favoured with. From his long experience in the business he feels confident that he is capable of ensuring the greatest satisfaction. Slate and metal Billiard

T.P. O'Connor.

Tables with improved rubber cushions, cast-iron frames and adjusting screws, made to order. Balls, cues, marking boards supplied. Cushions re-stuffed, etc.

By 1901, No.10 Castle Street was described as 'untenanted premises' but was still known colloquially as 'O'Connor's Billiard Rooms'. In July that year, he was offering for sale 'a spacious house, including shop and yard at Castle Street' which was held under a lease dated 1 March 1705. The advertisement stated that 'Mrs O'Connor's term expires on 25 March 1904' and that the premises had been unoccupied for some time past. It had what was described as 'a fine lock-up yard with outhouses and a gate entrance in Castle Street'.

When the property failed to sell, it was eventually auctioned in September 1901 by Mr O'Ferrall in Fry Place. It was described as the birthplace of T.P. O'Connor MP. The bidding commenced at £50 and it was knocked down to Mr J.J. Hynes at the sum of £150.

In 1928, the old building was demolished and a new one built in its place. In the 1929 Election, T.P. O'Connor, who was the 'Father of the House of Commons' was returned. He was wheeled in to the House of Commons to take the Oath but this was to be his last visit to the House. He was by now in his eighty-second year; he had become frail and his mobility was severely limited. In August he wrote, 'I am told by everybody that I may live for years yet. Personally, a nice quiet passing away in my sleep is the ideal I most long for, but things do not seem to happen that way.' He attended the Royal Garden Party and exchanged pleasantries with Lloyd George and later threw in the towel as a contributor to *T.P.'s Weekly*, or *T.P. & Cassell's Weekly* as it then was, thus ending a journalistic career which had spanned six decades. On Monday 18 November 1929, he died. A political friend described his death, saying it was 'as he would have wished to die … he suffered no pain, judging by his expression and his smile when I left him. He was quite happy, in possession of all his faculties, and fully conscious. He received the last rites of the Church.' T.P. O'Connor was buried at Kensal Green following a Requiem Mass in Westminster Cathedral.

Plaque Unveiled in his Memory

A plaque was unveiled on No.10 Castle Street by the Rt Hon. Alfred Byrne TD, Lord Mayor of Dublin, on Sunday 18 July 1937. Alfie Byrne (1882-1956) was a Nationalist politician who

had served in the House of Commons as MP for the Harbour
Division of Dublin (1914-18). He was many times made Lord
Mayor of Dublin, and indeed, was possibly the most popular
Lord Mayor the capital has ever had. After Irish independence, he
served as an independent TD for various Dublin constituencies
(1923-28, 1931-56), and while he was not in the Dáil, he spent
three years or so in the Senate. He was asked by the Athlone
Development Association to unveil the plaque to T.P. and this he
readily did. One wonders did he notice that one of the dates on
the plaque was incorrect? The members of Athlone Development
Association at that time were: John Grenham; Kitty Kilkelly;
P.J. O'Connor, PC, UDC (honorary secretary); J.M. Huban; H.
Feeley, NT, Kiltoom; P.C. Molloy, NT, Clonmacnoise; Sean O'
Hurley; M. Martin; A. Taylor; P.J. Coughlan; W. Ring; P. Murphy;
C. Devine; J.J. Lynch; M. Butler; P. Hanley; James Geraghty; M.
Murray, and Malachy Kelly. This same committee was responsible
for erecting the plaque to John Count McCormack in the Bawn.

Tormey & Co. Solicitors

In 1958, permission was granted to Mr W.A. Tormey to erect
an office at the rear of his house in Castle Street. Later, when
the Tormey family home was moved to Hodson Bay, the entire
building was converted to use as offices. The Tormey connection with the firm lasted until Billy Tormey, a popular Athlone
solicitor who had served his time with the late Mr D.J. Hannon,
became a District Justice in 1968. He later lived in Mullingar.

The practice, which has grown to become one of the major
solicitors' practices in Athlone, has been under the watchful eye
of Barra Flynn for many years. A highlight in the local educational calendar is the awarding of the Tormey & Co. scholarship
to a young student of law. Some years ago, Barra Flynn was also
responsible for the commissioning of a second piece of sculpture
to commemorate T.P.'s links with No. 10 Castle Street.

16

The Last Days of the Old Bridge of Athlone

We beg leave to draw the attention of the Vice-Sovereign to the state of our bridge on Market Days whereby lives are seriously endangered by the manner in which it is blocked up with carts. Could not a remedy be effected by placing a policeman or two on either side of the bridge whose duty it would be not to allow cars or carriages to pass from one side to the other except in turn and in train allowing a certain time for their crossing from the Roscommon side to the Westmeath side and vice versa.

19 February 1834

This extract, and the two that follow, relate to the Elizabethan bridge of Athlone, which was notoriously narrow. It was the bridge which featured in the Sieges of Athlone and which, though virtually destroyed, was repaired and served for a further century and a half before it was eventually replaced during the Shannon Navigation works of the 1840s.

Simpleton Crushed

This day a poor simpleton, named Thomas Gormley, was passing over the bridge when the cars of some coal porters pressed him so closely to the battlements as to injure him very seriously. The coal porters are in custody and it is not certain that the poor fellow will recover.

5 January 1838

Near Drowning

On Saturday last 26th ult. as a young countryman was attempting to get over the bridge from the Connaught to the Leinster side and finding it, as ever on Market Days, wholly impossible. For hours he ventured to walk on the low, rugged and broken battlements, north side, in order to facilitate his progress, when two cars coming in contact the end of a sack on the car next to him toppled him into the river for a length of thirty feet at least. Fortunately the man fell opposite the middle arch where the current is exceedingly rapid and sufficiently deep to break the velocity of the fall before he got to the bottom which is covered with stones. He was instantly swept on by the waters which now and then overwhelmed him a distance of five hundred yards when a turf cot, attracted by people on the bridge shouting as if each minute was to be the sufferer's last – put out and reached him in time to save him from a premature and watery grave. The poor fellow was much fatigued and nearly exhausted when he was taken to land.

1 February 1839

The turf cot referred to was a long shallow draft vessel, which was once a very common sight on the Shannon at Athlone. The Shannon cot was used to transfer goods such as hay, potatoes and turf from places such as Clonown and Clonbonny upriver to the markets in Athlone. Michael Fallon, writing in a book on Clonown, described the cot as being 'two and a half metres wide and six metres long'. Cots were also used to transport the coffin for funerals going across the river to Clonmacnoise, and for ferrying livestock from farm to farm. The cot was propelled through the shallow waters by pole and was rowed through deeper waters.

The New Bridge

The first stone of the new bridge about to be built here was, on this day, laid in the eastern abutment by Mr Buck, the district engineer. The ceremony was completely confined to those immediately connected with the work. Mr Long the resident engineer, Mr McMahon the contractor and his agent Mr Wrothely being the only ones present with the exception of the workmen.

5 November 1841

All the workmen and persons employed in the prepara-tory work for the construction of the bridge have struck for an increase in wages on Monday last. All now is stillness and stagnation where up to this has been the bustle of active employment.

30 April 1842

The foundation for the last abutment [of the new bridge] was completed last week. Preparations are now being made for commencing the superstructure – the centre frames for one of the new arches have already been erected. The quay walls below the bridge have advanced considerably. The piling of the Coffer Dam below the bridge, where the river is to be exca-vated for a lock [and weir] across the river is near completion. There are about 550 men receiving daily employment at the works. Mr Long is the resident engineer.

18 August 1843

The contractors for the quay and lock at Athlone have made it a practice to pay the men in their employment monthly to force them to purchase goods in the stores they themselves have established on the ground at a great deal a dearer rate than they could purchase them elsewhere.

25 August 1843

Accident at the Docks

A young man named Smyth was working at the Docks here drove a barrow against the large railway wagon which tho' loaded at the time had not the crank in it, when the wagon fell back and buried Smyth beneath a heap of rubbish and stones. He is dreadfully crushed and there is little hope of his recovery. This is the fourth one who has been hurt here within the past few weeks, one of whom had his head so much lacerated that he died of lockjaw.

25 August 1843

Water Wheel Experiment

On Tuesday we had much pleasure in witnessing the experiment of the water wheel to unwatering the Coffer dam for the erection of the lock in this town, one wheel but two pumps. They are of oblong form being one foot five by one foot eight with six feet of a stroke, the wheel working the pumps twenty strokes per minute and throwing the incredible quantity of 1,700 gallons of water per minute. They sunk the water in the coffer dam, which is 320 feet long by 120 feet broad, in about nine hours notwithstanding that there are a great many sewers running into it when they stopped the water being sufficiently sunk to fasten the first tier of braces. The wheel was executed under the superintendence of Mr James Mullins. There is also a second wheel to which other pumps are to be attached and there is not the slightest doubt that when all the arrangements are perfected that no body of water no matter however great will be able to impede the progress of the work the more particularly as the dam is perfectly staunch.

19 January 1844

Some years ago, when the site was being prepared for the modern St Peter's Port housing development, a very large stone wheel was unearthed. Our best guess at the time was that the wheel had been used to power cutting equipment to prepare the cut stone for the docks. However, it now seems much more likely that it was used in the operation outlined above. Unfortunately, the stone, which was an integral part of the industrial history of Athlone, was, I understand, removed by a foreman or workman on the site to adorn his garden.

The bridge of Athlone, which was built in 1844.

Farewell to the Bridge

The old bridge was blown up yesterday from powder lowered into the apertures and fuses arranged. At 4.30 matches were applied to each pier successively and no vestige of many of the arches are to be seen. The ruins will be cleared as soon as the water is low enough to commence the deepening of the river. Sufficient remains at present to give the ruins a strikingly picturesque appearance when viewed from its rival, the new bridge, which now adorns our town.

19 January 1844

The new bridge referred to is, of course, the present town bridge, which was officially opened in November 1844, heralding a new era in the history of Athlone.

17

The Actress and
the Candlestick

One of the more unusual cases to come before the court in Athlone in 1898 must surely have been the case of Mrs Aubrey, an actress, who, while staying in Athlone, was sharing lodging rooms with her husband, Mr Jack Aubrey, himself an actor, somewhere in the Main Street area. On 11 June, Mrs Aubrey was brought to the local court to appear before Captain Preston RM due to a domestic disturbance. It appears that hostilities broke out in the small hours of the previous Saturday night and continued with periods of both calm and turmoil until the Monday, when the couple had a further row which eventually ended in blows. In fact, it was claimed that Mr Jack Aubrey had suffered two or three blows to the head from a candlestick wielded by his wife.

Having heard the preliminary case, Captain Preston turned to the defendant and said, 'I remand you.'

Mrs Aubrey: 'You what Messeur?'

Captain Preston: 'I remand you.'

Guard: 'It means, Ma'am, you must go to gaol for eight days.'

Mrs Aubrey: 'Oh no, dear Captain. I really could not do that. I could not sleep in a cell.'

However, taking no nonsense from the defendant, Captain Preston insisted that she serve her sentence and appear before him at the next sitting. Mrs Aubrey was allowed to see her husband, Jack, before she left Athlone to face eight days in the county gaol. According to the local newspaper, 'the farewell was as ardent as

Juliet's', but Jack, as Romeo, hardly came up to the mark, incipiently remarking as his Juliet was hurried away, 'It would be better the meeting was deferred to a more suitable occasion.'

The Actress in Trouble – Reconciliation

The next issue of the paper reported:

> Mrs Aubrey appeared in the police court on Monday morning and is a born daughter of the stage. The few pointed questions she addressed to Dr Shanley might have been the emanations of a senior counsel. She was somewhat incensed against Mr Aubrey whose evidence was, more or less, against her but was satisfied when Captain Preston with a certain delicacy suggested by way of a question whether friendly relations would in future exist between the disputants. Mrs Aubrey is still young and of emphatic disposition. When Captain Preston took his seat on the bench she walked to what is intended for a dock and armed with two or three letters listened to what was said against her. Mr J. Lyster joined Captain Preston a few minutes after the court was opened and Mrs Aubrey bombarded the injured Aubrey with the artillery of her eyes, while Mr Treacy read to her so formidable a charge as that she did unlawfully assault and cut John Aubrey causing him serious bodily injury. It is such an unusual thing to find an Ophelia in a position so strongly contrasted with the glare of the footlights that the spectacle attracted a large public attendance which included a professional man who is well known for the interest he takes in political, legal and social problems.
>
> Captain Preston, who ever holds evenly the beam of justice, interrogated the injured actor before depositions were taken. Then ascertaining that he was now well, though exhausted, the gravity of a determined assault somewhat disappeared from the proceedings and it was as if all in the Court had come to wit-

ness a reconciliation – which, however, was not effected until Aubrey let the Court know that he had cause to complain before, which was assailed with the exclamation 'You sweep', which was a comparatively mild expletive compared with the tragedienne glances which the accused shot at her bandaged husband.

The Medical Evidence

Dr Shanley, in evidence, stated that he was called to see Mr Aubrey on Saturday night week and found him in an exhausted state, having lost a quantity of blood. He had one wound over the forehead and another over the temple. One of the arteries of the head was cut. The wounds, he said, could have been caused by the parts of the dismembered candlestick which Mr Pearson produced for the benefit of the Court. The wounds at the outset were liable to become dangerous but the actor was now recovered.

Mrs Aubrey, raising the veil, turned to the doctor with the announcement that she would like to ask him a question. Dr Shanley looked as if he were up for the final examination of his younger days and had to demonstrate his knowledge of anatomy with a badly preserved mummy taken from the Greek hall a little after Cleopatra's time. Captain Preston, seeing the awkwardness of the situation, and the maze which a controversial argument on abstruse points of surgery was likely to lead to, turned to Mrs Aubrey saying, 'It must be a question arising out of the deposition.' Mrs Aubrey thought so herself too, for her questions were as pointed as the needle in a mariner's compass. 'Was the exhaustion entirely due to the cut?' was her searching question. 'I think so', replied Dr Shanley. 'May I ask another question? … was he not in a weak state before he met with the accident?'

'I did not see him before he met with the accident.'

'He was in a weak state for several weeks before,' she said, then she asked if he were perfectly sober.

Dr Shanley: 'I should say not, he appeared to have some drink taken.'

Mrs Aubrey: 'Did I not tell you he struck me before I raised the candlestick to him?'

Head Constable Clerkin: 'Yes, but it would take a short-hand writer to take down all you said. I observed that your eye was black.'

Mrs Aubrey: 'It is not all gone yet. I said I did not deliberately hit him with the candlestick. I threw it at him.'

Preston asked Aubrey if he were friendly disposed towards his wife. To which Aubrey replied, 'Perfectly so.'

Preston: 'So you don't contemplate further trouble or assault?'

Aubrey: 'I hope not. I have received a letter from a Company and it is very possible that they might arrange with me if my wife was at liberty.'

In view of the fact that the defendant had suffered a week's imprisonment, they were giving her the benefit of the First Offender's Act. The defendant was then discharged.

The Aubreys never came to the attention of the court in Athlone again and Captain Preston returned to his humdrum caseload of the trespass of cattle, breach of the licensing laws and petty larceny. However, one can be sure that when he looked back upon his career on the bench in Athlone, the case of the actress and the candlestick was one of the most novel and unusual cases which he had ever dealt with.

18

Mickey Hatter: Athlone's Last Bellman

The position of bellman in Athlone seems to have been introduced by the Athlone Town Commissioners in the 1840s. Initially, one of the principal duties assigned to him was to inform the people of the town of the dates and times of the meetings of the Commissioners.

In the 1890s, one Patrick Hehir was the town bellman. In 1894, he appeared before the local court charged with assault on Martin King. However, Hehir took out a cross-summons on Mr King and the outcome of the case was that the charges against Hehir were discharged while King had to pay a 5s fine and serve seven days in prison.

In March 1895, Hehir was before the courts again, this time charged with public drunkenness. It appears from the evidence that he had been going around the town for two or three hours and that he had visited a number of public houses. By six o'clock he was so drunk that he fell on the street and cried out, 'I'm drunk, arrest me.' An RIC man, Constable Rock, obliged, but Hehir didn't take too kindly to his intervention. When he appeared before the local court he was fined 20s and costs (or fourteen days' imprisonment) on the charge of drunkenness and two months' imprisonment for assault on Constable Rock. Hehir had been trying to muster up a decent 'welcome home' for a number of local youths who were before the court in Roscommon charged with assault on some street preachers.

In 1898, Mr Hehir appeared on a similar charge of assaulting a police officer and received a two-month custodial sentence.

After Hehir's day, Athlone Urban District Council appointed one John Crowley to the post of bellman, but at this stage it seems that there was a fine line between this official bellman and others who considered themselves '*bona fides*'. Mr Crowley was employed in 1902 and in the course of the discussion at the council meeting it was agreed that he should be given a badge and a hat and a new suit of clothes. It was also agreed that he should be empowered to prevent anyone else from 'ringing' and to use the Town Hall as his official address. However, Mr Crowley's tenure of office was short, as the famous Tom (Picinnini) Ward soon entered the fray.

The Post of Bellman is Diminished

In the early years of the twentieth century, the post of bellman seems to have been diminished and this is evidenced by the fact that there was open competition among 'criers'.

In 1903, Picinnini Ward, a local bill poster and bell-ringer, appeared at a council meeting and asked to be given a uniform as town bellman. His request was met with laughter. Councillor Galvin asked him, 'Will you want a cocked hat?' to which question there was further laughter, but Mr Ward, undaunted, stated, 'Ye promised to give them to me and I'd wear them everyday barrin' Sunday.' Again, there was great hilarity in the Council Chamber until the Council Chairman told Ward to 'go about his business'.

In October 1908, there were two applicants for the post: Michael Hehir, with an address of Moynan's Row, and John Harnett of College Lane. Both felt entitled to the post because of their fathers' long service. Tom (Picinnini) Ward let it be known that he too should be employed. Whether any or all of them were ever accredited with official status is uncertain, but what is certain is that both Hehir and Ward took to the streets and began a rivalry which was to become legendary.

Mickey Hatter

In July 1916, a correspondent writing to the *Westmeath Independent* reported on a novelty 'Cinema and Variety' item which he attended in the Longworth Hall in Northgate Street. He wrote, 'Seeing the Athlone Bellman displaying his noble proportions in the Ormond–Dawn, livery, cut away coat, brass buttons, knee breeches and tall hat reminds one of the time when most of the borough towns in Ireland had their livery in distinctive colours.' One can only speculate as to whether this was the famous Mickey Hatter at the zenith of his career. Certainly Mickey was the best remembered bellman of old Athlone.

The name Mickey Hatter was a corruption of Michael Hehir and he was the son of Patrick Hehir, who held the office in the 1890s. Mickey had two bells; the larger one was rung to announce commercial ventures such as the pictures, operas, plays and concerts, and the smaller, official bell, was used to announce official Urban Council business including water cuts, gas cuts and the likes.

In the absence of an official uniform, Mickey was forced to wear a 1798 costume which had been bequeathed to him by the St Patrick's League Dramatic Society. In 1929, Mickey was still trying to ascertain whether or not he was the town bellman. In a letter addressed to the council he stated, 'I still feel obliged if ye would kindly let me know who is the principal bell-ringer and bill-poster in Athlone.' Mickey was writing from his home in Bastion Street and concluded, 'Anyone can come along at present and put up bills and notices everywhere and anywhere they like. My father was bill-poster and bell-ringer in this town and was supplied with a cap by the Council.'

Mickey Hatter *vs* Picinnini Ward

While Mickey Hatter held sway on his own side of town and made the announcements for the Urban District Council, his rival Tom (Picinnini) Ward (who was employed by the Garden Vale Cinema) felt that he was the official bellman for the Leinster side of the town. Both characters were considered to be quite inoffensive, but some locals decided to stir up rivalry between them. Ward was perhaps the better dressed, as he delighted in wearing his official livery of chocolate-brown coat with gold braid.

In time, Mickey Hatter became so incensed by the rivalry that he drew a line across the town bridge and challenged Ward, 'If you dare to cross I'll hit you on the head with my bell.' Tom Ward complained to his employer, who in turn complained to the police. Mickey Hatter was cautioned that he could not take such action and that if he did he would be charged with assault. When Ward was feeling brave he would venture across to the Connaught side to 'cry' the pictures in the Garden Vale Cinema, but as soon as Mickey heard that he had infiltrated his territory, he would be out ringing his bell, trying to drown out the opposition. Eventually a solution was found by his employers, who provided Tom Ward with a cart with the cinema posters stuck on a triangular frame. From then on, Picinnini was able to go around the town advertising his wares without ever having to say a word.

And so it was that Mickey Hatter was the last official bellman of Athlone, having successfully silenced the opposition. When he died in May 1945, the *Westmeath Independent* announced the death of one of 'Athlone's best known and most colourful personalities'. It recalled that when Athlone rode high in the realms of soccer, his pride in the hometown team found an outlet in his popular and familiar cry, 'Athlone, hold your own.' Sadly, however, only a dozen or so turned up for his funeral to Cornamagh cemetery.

19

The Market Square

Among the most popular series of articles I have written over the years have been my edited versions of taped interviews with Jimmy O'Connor, dealing the Connaught side of Athlone. Jimmy O'Connor, who has now completed over four score years and ten, is blessed with a remarkable memory, and recalled details from the 1920s and '30s. I have tried from the papers of my father, the late Brendan O'Brien, and other sources, to give some idea of the earlier and later histories of some of the premises which Jimmy talks about, thus helping to put down on paper some of the twentieth-century history of the streets and businesses of Athlone. This is an edited version of the four articles in this series which recorded the history of the Market Square.

The premises now known as the Liturgical Centre, occupied by the Sister Disciples of the Divine Master, incorporates three earlier business houses. The first was Finnerty's. This premises, which was a well-known 'watering hole' for the islanders from Lough Ree, was run by the Finnerty family, including Jack Finnerty, who was a renowned Athlone footballer. As well as the licensed premises, they dealt in animal feeding stuffs and ran a very good shop. No.9 Castle Street, the premises later occupied by Finnerty, was occupied by Thomas Geraghty from 1867 until his death in 1907. In 1907, Bernard Finnerty and his wife Norah took over this business and the Finnerty name was retained until the premises were offered for sale in 1982. In the 1960s, after the

The Market Square, early twentieth century.

death of Mrs Finnerty, the licence was transferred to her daughter, Mrs Catherine Mary Gallagher. This old-world pub, which retained much of its earlier charm, was used in the filming of RTÉ's *Caught in the Free State*, which was based on the story of the German spies who were held in Custume Barracks during the Second World War.

Mr Tommy Gallagher

Mr Tommy Gallagher, who lived at No.9 Castle Street, was something of a local legend. Tommy, whose father was the caretaker of the Fr Mathew Hall, married Kitty Finnerty in 1939. He was an employee of the ESB from 1928 until his death in 1973. He had a long and distinguished career as a cox with Athlone Boat Club and was regarded as an excellent rowing coach – Athlone Boat Club has a boat named in his memory. He held various positions in Athlone Yacht Club, including rear admiral and honorary secretary. He successfully built several boats, including a twelve-foot sailing boat and a fourteen-footer of the IDRA design, which won for him first place in Ireland for the best amateur-built boat at Dunmore East Regatta in 1950. Two years later he built a Shannon One Design, becoming the first amateur to success-fully build this class of sailing boat. He sailed in regattas both on Lough Ree and Lough Derg. Apart from his interest in sailing and rowing, he had an abiding interest in stage management and served both the Athlone Musical Society and the Athlone Little Theatre very faithfully for many years. He was also a founder member of the Old Athlone Society, but perhaps his greatest claim to fame is that he built himself a television set – based on the original Baird system – as early as 1934 and was receiving clear signals from Crystal Palace, London long before commercial television came to the Irish midlands.

Next to Finnerty's were the Egans, who ran a sweet shop, 'there was Miss Josie and Miss Mary Egan there and many's the penny-worth of sweets I bought there as a schoolboy'. The sweets they stocked were NKM's (North Kerry Manufactures), which were sold ten for a penny. They also sold a beautiful range of biscuits as well as cigarettes and tobacco. Josie Egan later married Mr P.J. Boushell, who was manager of the Palace Bar and also ran a shop in Custume Place. Jack Boushell ran the Castle Cake Shop in the 1960s. It had originally opened in 1950, with Kitty Higgins of Connaught Street as the proprietor. In 1969, when it was sold, it became the Liturgical Centre and the Sister Disciples of the Divine Master remained here until 1983, when they moved down to Main Street in order for the old premises to be demolished and the new Liturgical Centre built.

Next door to Egans was Barnes, although the name Maher was above the door. I believe the families were connected. They had a delph shop here and Paddy Barnes, who worked as a traveller, was an uncle of the great Colm Barnes, who started Glen Abbey Textiles in Dublin, which was famous for 'Bradmola' silk stock-ings, amongst other products. Among the specialities in Barnes's were 'Celtic transfers' suitable for use on Irish dancing costumes, as well as a range of 'lined traced needle-work and embroidery treads'.

These three premises – Finnerty's, Egan's and Barnes's have been subsumed into the present Liturgical Centre premises. Here, the Sisters Disciples of the Divine Master, who first came to Athlone in the 1960s to a convent in Ballykeeran, established their new convent in 1986. Attached to the convent is an excellent outlet for the sale of cards and religious goods, as well as a wonderful oasis of peace and tranquillity in their Chapel of Adoration. The order was founded by Fr James Alberioni from the north of Italy. Fr James established ten religious orders, each with its own particular area of endeavour. The first Irish novice to join the order was Sr Muriel Fetherston, a native of Athlone, and many have joined since, including Sr Louise O'Rourke, another Athlone native.

The Castle Gift Shop

Jimmy O'Connor remembers the premises next door to the Liturgical Centre as Donnelly's. In the late 1920s and early '30s, there was a Mrs Donnelly here who was connected to 'Donnelly's of the Hollow', as the premises now known as Sean's Bar was then called. She ran a butcher's shop, and in June 1932 she applied for a licence to slaughter animals in the premises of Mrs Hughes in Main Street. Before this was Donnelly's it was a sweetshop run by Mrs Margaret Kilkelly, whose husband Frank Kilkelly was a brother of Councillor Michael Kilkelly in Clonmel. The Kilkellys emigrated and Mrs Kilkelly died in New York in 1951.

In the 1930s, Martin Flanagan opened a clothes shop here. His advertisement in this newspaper on 15 September 1934 read, 'Flanagan's Shirt and Hosiery Specialist opening next Friday, 21 September. Shirts, Pyjamas, Underwear, Ties, Kerchiefs, Hosiery, Slipovers, Cardigans, etc. 7 Castle Street.' For forty years this business operated from this premises – one of their specialities was the sale of wool – until an announcement appeared in this paper on 14 January 1972, 'Mr Martin Flanagan, Castle Street, who is shortly retiring from business would like to thank his customers for support over the years.'

When it was offered for sale, it was bought by the late Gerry Gray, a lecturer and Head of School in Athlone Regional College, who opened one of Athlone's first bookshops here. The College Bookshop, which was run by Mrs Claire Gray and her daughters, was located here from 1972 to 1974, when the business was transferred to Athlone Shopping Centre. The premises was then acquired by Gerald and Eileen Dowling, who incorporated it into their new newsagency, which also incorporated Miss Francie Dolan's shop. This newsagent and tobacconist shop was very successful for many years. In turn, Gerry Dowling sold his business to the Donovan family, who carried out their business here for some years. Since 1991 it has been run as a highly successful newsagency and fancy goods shop by Ms Dympna Earley.

Alford the Barber

When Messrs J.J. and E. Hynds were disposing of their two properties in Castle Street in 1905, one was sold to Thomas Coffey while the other was acquired by J.C. Alford. To begin with, Alford was advertising an umbrella making, recovering and repair service – with prices of 1s 6d for ladies' and 1s 9d for gents' umbrellas.

By 1907, Alford was advertising his services as a barber. His adverts asked the question, 'How does Alford cut hair?' to which the reply was, 'As you like it – William Shakespeare', and this slogan was a regular feature of his advertising for many years. Jimmy O'Connor recalls that these premises were occupied by Alfords until the late 1950s. Mr Alford had a daughter who looked after him. He was an Englishman and when he retired he returned to England. Billy Hughes, who was a barber in Alford's, took over the business and continued there until his untimely death in 1965.

The premises were later incorporated, with Butler's next door, to form the Thatch Bar, which was developed by Jim and Liz Kearns.

Butler's

Jimmy recalls Butler's as a unique shop which stocked feeding stuffs for farmers and had a licensed premises attached to it. This was a very popular bar which was very well run by the Butler brothers, Michael and Eamon. Mr Edmund Butler was a cage-bird fancier, who kept canaries and other cage birds, and so this was perhaps the only shop in Athlone which stocked bird seed and other supplies for those who kept caged birds.

These premises were once occupied by Farrell, an old, established family grocer who stocked tea, wines, spirits and provisions. In 1910, William Kerrigan, who acquired the licence from Mrs Anne Farrell, was an agent for various shipping companies, including White Star, American and Dominion Line. He was also an insurance agent. An advertisement for Kerrigan's in 1913 read:

Butler's of the Square with shop-hands Joe Tell and Mary Walsh.

> W.J. Kerrigan, The Square, Athlone
> (opposite the Castle)
> Groceries, fruits & provisions, wines, whiskies, porter in the
> pink of condition

Best house in town for cooked meats, sandwiches, pork-pies, sweets and ales of every description. Turkeys and geese to order. All brands of high class tobacco, cigars and cigarettes, pipes and pocket knives in great variety from 2*d* each. Combs, perfumes and patent medicines.

Agents for all steamship lines, passengers booked to all parts of the world, assisted passages arranged to Australia and Canada, employment guaranteed on arrival, traveller's luggage insured at cheapest rates and for any length of time. Portmanteaus, trunks and suit cases from 2*s* 6*d* each. Baskets from 6*d* each. Walking sticks and Irish souvenirs kept.

According to the late Gilbert Hughes of Coosan, Willie Kerrigan was known as 'Lady' Kerrigan; he was a native of Galway, 'a real lady killer' and a talented amateur actor.

By 1915, Edmund Butler, a native of Brideswell, had taken over from Willie Kerrigan. He had plenty of business experience, having spent upwards of eighteen years working in Limerick and some time in Wales before returning to work in Athlone.

Winters and Coffey

Jimmy O'Connor recalls the predecessors to The Square House as Winters and Coffey's. It is probably worth stating that this business had earlier (from about 1898) been John Kennedy's Drapery Warehouse and as such we can say that The Square House continues in business here, in the twenty-first century, in a line of trade which was first established in the late nineteenth century.

Mrs Hogan, who ran the antique shop with her son Michael for many years, was a member of the Kennedy family.

John Kennedy was one of the leading drapers on the Connaught side of Athlone, and in 1906 his was the only shop in Athlone where the assistants got a half-day on a Thursday – a practice that became widespread in later years. Kennedy's carried a wide and varied range of goods as an advertisement of 1904 testifies, 'Sale of millinery, mantles, jackets, ladies shirts and blouses, under-clothing, prints, dresses and costumes. Men's, boys' and youths' suits, boots, shoes, hats, caps, collars, ties, etc.'

When John Kennedy retired in 1924, Joseph Winters and Patrick Coffey purchased his interest in the business, and opened their new concern on 11 April that year. The nature of the business was a Ladies & Gents Outfitters. Jimmy O'Connor remembers Mr Winters as 'a very nice gentleman who always wore a wide-brimmed hat'. The partnership was dissolved in 1932 and Mr Winters went to the west of Ireland, where he opened up on his own. Paddy Coffey continued in business until 1958, when a well-known businessman, Patrick Pettit of Ballygar, took over the premises as a going concern.

In January 1962, the late Mr Andrew O'Connor, who had premises in Main Street, took over the business and relocated The Square House to its present location. For over forty years the O'Connor family have provided a first-class family-run business. In recent years, they downsized their main premises and made an extra business unit available; initially it was occupied by a hearing aid service but now it houses the Head, Shoulders, Knees & Toes holistic treatment centre, providing much-needed relief from the stresses and strains of daily life, as well as a first-class beautician's service for the fairer sex.

P.J. Byrne's

Next door to The Square House was P.J. Byrne's. Jimmy O'Connor, though only a boy at the time, recalls hearing that this establishment started out as Byrne, O'Halloran & Co. P.J. Byrne of Baylough had been an employee of Messrs Lysters, serving as foreman of the furniture department before going into partnership with Mr O'Halloran. As an adult, Jimmy knew both gentlemen well – P.J. Byrne from his business in the Square and Denis O'Halloran, who later opened up his own business in Custume Place in the premises which later became the Genoa Bar.

When P.J. Byrne left Lyster's, he was replaced by Mr William McCrea, a Donegal man who was very popular, a scout leader and a member of the St Mary's Hall Committee. In the mid-1930s, Mr McCrea died young and Jimmy O'Connor's brother Michael took over the furniture department. William McCrea's brother Alfie came to Athlone in the '20s and was a long-serving employee of Lyster's. Byrne literally left his mark in Lyster's because Jimmy O'Connor recalls the initials 'P.J.B.' cut into the banisters of the back stairs leading to the furniture department.

When Byrne and O'Halloran opened in October 1922, the advertisement read:

New Opening!!! Byrne O'Halloran & Co. will open at the Square, Athlone a general hardware and furnishing warehouse on Friday 6 October. Paints, oils and ironmongery of all descriptions stocked. A trial solicited – all goods lowest prices. Motto – satisfaction and courtesy.

The partnership between Byrne and O'Halloran was short-lived, but P.J. Byrne continued in business for many years until he retired in the 1960s. He died in 1971 and his widow, Margaret, died in 1978. The shop was run by his son Padraig until recent times. This was one of the legendary shops of old Athlone; a place where anything from a needle to an anchor could be found.

When Padraig and his wife retired, the shop was acquired by the Palace Bar and demolished to facilitate the building of a modern bar and lounge.

J. Dixon & Sons

Before Jimmy O'Connor's time, this premises, which was once the Central Hotel owned by the Geraghty family, was occupied by Dixon & Sons. The Dixons were associated with the business life of Athlone from the 1850s at least, when John Dixon was a boot merchant in Main Street. John later diversified and became a seed merchant, and by 1903 the family had moved their business to the Square. From their extensive premises in the Square the Dixons added many new lines to their business – animal feeds, coal, oils, brushes, general hardware and leather goods were added to their core products of boots, shoes and seeds.

It is said that the Dixons, who were a non-Catholic family, were alarmed by the burnings of a number of big houses in the vicinity of Athlone. In July 1922, they retired from business and the premises were offered for sale by Michael O'Ferrall, auctioneer in Fry Place.

I will leave it to another old Athlonian, Mr Michael Kilkelly, writing in the *Westmeath Independant* some seventy years ago, to describe the premises as he remembered it in his youth:

In Castle Street, where Mr Byrne's house furnishing warehouse now stands there was, formerly, a rather large house which was occupied by weekly tenants in all its rooms. An open passageway led to the back area in which there were several small tenements and in which lived some well-known, humble people. Their names were Kathy and Mary Egan, fruit sellers, whose stand was always at the corner of the bridge next to the castle; 'Honny' Plunkett, vegetable dealer; Biddy Glavey known as 'Biddy Five Thumbs' and James Kilroy, paperhanger. On the first floor of the outer premises was the shaving and hairdressing salon of a well-known man, popularly called 'Carr, the barber' who was humorous but harmless. The place (back and front) was always called 'Little Hell' until Mr George Everard demolished it and built the fine warehouse as it now stands. After Mr Everard's death, Miss Jane Geraghty carried on a fine drapery business and later on herself and her sister kept the branch post office in O'Connell Street.

The Palace Bar

This premises, at the corner of Castle Street and Barrack Street, occupies what has long been considered an important and pivotal site, and is perhaps one of the best-located public houses in the town of Athlone. The site has a long tradition not only with the sale of alcohol, but in the eighteenth century was, at different times, the location of a brew house and distillery. Edward Mabbott had a brew house in the back of the premises in 1730; in the period 1740-5 it was occupied by Robert Codnor, a distiller, and by 1766 the occupier was another prominent brewer and distiller, Thomas Hovendon. In 1784, Hovendon had a brewery here and a distillery off Connaught Street near the canal.

From the mid-nineteenth century this was George Everard's, but around 1885 it was taken over by Luke and Peter Watson and 'remodelled' to become 'the spacious Palace Bar'. We can assume that it was the Watsons who introduced the name and that Edward Coen, publican, retained the name when he took over in 1893.

The first manager of the Palace Bar that Jimmy O'Connor remembers was Mr Patrick Boushell in the 1920s. He left in 1928 to take over the tobacconist, confectionery and newspaper business in Church Street which had been run by Mr P. O'Neill. During Mr Bushell's time there were two brothers on the staff of the Palace Bar who lived-in, and they were Vincent and Michael Walsh. Michael was a great cyclist and Vincent later took over Carthy's, before going out to take over a public house in Brideswell, which he ran for many years. Another popular manager of the Palace Bar was Mr Michael Hanly, who Jimmy remembers as a nice gentleman and 'a great man for St Peter's parish'.

The Markets

Before we leave the Market Square I want to tell you about the wonderful markets which used to be held here. There was a small market house, a little wooden structure in the middle of the Square with a weighbridge beside it. On the chapel side of the Square was a tripod for weighing hundred-weights of potatoes, turnips, etc.

When farmers brought their produce to the market they had to register their loads. The weighbridge could take a cart but not a motor vehicle; as far as I remember the plate was about 6'6" square. The official on duty knew the weight of each empty cart and could therefore work out the weight of produce brought to the market.

In the weigh house they kept the weights – a hundred-weight, two hundred-weights, fifty-six pounds, two stone, a stone and half a stone – and these were used on the frames when they were weighing goods on the tripod. They put the spuds or other commodities on one side and they put the weights on the other side and once it balanced you knew you were getting the correct weight.

In the old days the whole place was chock-a-block with carts: ponies' carts, horses' carts, donkeys' carts, and even down to Main Street and the back of the castle there were farmers selling the wares – vegetables, potatoes, etc. Athlone market was a great market and then you had Dublin hawkers that came from time to time selling all sorts of hardware and bargain goods. There was also a clothes market with stalls selling second-hand clothes. All the old country people, the women in shawls, would be from where the seat is near the castle right around to Main Street, selling butter and eggs (both duck eggs and hen eggs), and rabbits were a great go at that time also. You could by a pair of rabbits in the early thirties for 2s. Rabbits were regarded as a great delicacy and apart from the nice meat itself they made great soup.

Cheap Meat

I remember a butcher's stall – people tell me I don't but I do – it was at the path near where the old public toilet stood. He always had the same stand and he came up from Ballinasloe or Mount Bellew to sell his meat. In the late '20s and early '30s there was no refrigeration and especially in the summertime there would be huge bluebottles flying around the meat and still the people bought the meat and passed no remarks on it. You could get a pound of round steak in the shops for 10d and sirloin steak for 1s 3d a pound but from the butcher in the Square they cost 8d and 1s 0d respectively.

Before I finish on the markets, I just want to mention the three-quarts can. The three-quart can was a sweet can used for delivering boiled sweets to the shops. The shopkeepers decanted the sweets from the can into the glass jars for display and sale, and the three-quart can came into its own at the market in Athlone as a measure for potatoes. The can had a wire handle and when the farmer would fill the can with potatoes and build them up castle-like to the handle, you had a half a stone of potatoes. The customers brought their own canvas bags or baskets to the markets but they always got the fill of the three-quart can if they wanted a half a stone of potatoes.

The Lime Sellers

There were many people around who burned lime, especially in the Bealnamullia area of Athlone. The Lime Market was near the present pedestrian crossing at the top of the Accommodation Road. Here you could get a bucket of lime for 6*d*. This was used extensively by people to whitewash their houses or yards. I remember a lot of whitewashed houses in Lyster Street and Chapel Street. When you bought your bucket of lime you had to add water and 'blue' to make a good whitewash.

Those who came into town on a Fair Day could get a meal at a reasonable price in a special restaurant run to serve the needs of the farming community. A full dinner cost about 1*s* 6*d* whereas a simple meal such as a mug of tea and a sandwich cost about 6*d*. In Mardyke Street also there were places which served dinners on Fair Days.

To clean up after the Fairs and Markets, Mr Murphy from Brideswell Street came out with his horse-drawn watering cart. When he turned a lever it sprayed out water on each side and a couple of lads with brushes would sweep away all the debris from the streets.

There was a pig-fair every month and all the jobbers or 'the bacon men' as they were called used to come and buy pigs for the factories. There was one distinguishing feature of 'the bacon men' and that was that they all wore bright brown boots.

20

Anthony Trollope and Athlone

The British novelist Anthony Trollope (1815-1882) started his Irish career as Deputy Postal Surveyor in Banagher, County Offaly. When he arrived there in 1841 he first stayed in the Shannon Hotel. His Irish experiences, and particularly his experiences in Banagher, were to play a major role in his development as a novelist. This is why the town of Banagher is still today such an attraction for Trollope fans. In fact, his biographer, the late James Pope Hennessy, visited Banagher in 1970 and spent some time living in the Shannon Hotel and walking in the steps of the master.

The house in which Anthony Trollope later lived in Banagher, to the right of the old post office which was demolished in 1984, is still a major attraction in the town. It was while living in Banagher that he worked on his first novel, *The MacDermots of Ballycloran*, which was set in Leitrim and published in 1844. Trollope himself considered *The MacDermots* his best book and it has been described as 'one of the most melancholy books ever written'. Anthony Trollope married an Englishwoman, Rose Heseltine, in 1844 and the following year they went to live in Clonmel, where they lived until 1859. Of his time in Ireland Trollope wrote in his autobiography:

> It was altogether a very jolly life that I led in Ireland. The Irish people did not murder me, nor did they even break my head. I soon found them to be good-humoured, clever – the work-

ing classes very much more intelligent than those of England
– economical and hospitable.

Today, Trollope is still one of the most widely read Victorian
authors, and television adaptations of *The Barchester Chronicles*,
The Pallisers and *The Way We Live Now* have helped to introduce a
new generation of enthusiastic readers to his works.

Trollope's major Irish works, inspired by his eighteen-year
sojourn in this country (four years in Banagher and fourteen
years in Clonmel), are *The MacDermots of Ballycloran*, *The Kellys
and the O'Kellys*, *Castle Richmond*, *Phineas Finn*, *Phineas Redux* and
The Land Leaguers. An article on Trollope published in *The Dublin
Review* in 1872 claimed that, though an Englishman:

> [Trollope] writes a story as true to the saddest and heaviest
> truths of Irish life, as racy as the soil, as rich with the peculiar
> humour, the moral features, the social oddities, the subtle indi-
> viduality of the far west of Ireland as George Elliot's novels are
> true to the truths of English life.

Unfortunately we cannot claim that Anthony Trollope was
greatly influenced or indeed greatly impressed by Athlone, but he
was brought to the town in his official capacity as an inspector of
the Postal Service to examine the case of Burke the letter carrier.

The Case of James Burke

It seems that James Burke, a local letter carrier (or postman) in
Athlone, had grave difficulties in delivering the post to the correct addresses. Indeed it was claimed publicly that the man was
illiterate, and in January 1842, only four months after his arrival in
Banagher, Anthony Trollope was dispatched to Athlone to inves-
tigate the case. The investigation took place, the complaints were
heard and the letter carrier was tested for competency.

Anthony Trollope, English novelist, in old age. (© Mary Evans)

At the end of the inquiry Anthony Trollope concluded that James Burke was a fit person to carry out the task of letter carrier and he was allowed to return to work. However, all was not well. The original complainant was one Thomas Glynn of Victoria Place. Not satisfied with the verdict reached by Mr Trollope, Glynn wrote an open letter to Mr Augustus Godly, the secretary of the General Post Office in Dublin, which was published in *The Athlone Mirror* of 8 January 1842, in which he complained about the postal services in the town:

Athlone, 2 January 1842.

Dear Sir,

A gentleman from the Post Office attended here yesterday for the purpose of holding an investigation into the competency of James Burke letter carrier …
This enquiry seemed to me to be anything but satisfactory; however I sent you a letter, given to me THIS day by Burke, which will give you an idea of Burke's fitness for letter carrier, the thing speaks for itself.

I remain, Sir,
Your Obedient Servant,
Thomas Glynn

The enclosed letter was addressed to Mr Thomas Flynn, Dublin Gate Street, Athlone, but delivered to Mr Thomas Glynn at Victoria Place, Athlone.

Further Criticism

In a further letter to the editor of the *Athlone Mirror*, Thomas Glynn stated:

> Your advice no doubt is well intended but if the gross errors of the letter carrier are to be overlooked, and the public to be cajoled by a mock investigation, such as Mr Trollope held here on Saturday last (1 January, 1842) our best plan is to submit at once to the 'pranks of the orange letter carrier'. Whilst we find Mr Trollope ready to report him 'able to read', and instead of delivering a lecture to me on the 'serious responsibilities I incurred by not running around town after the peals of an orange post-man it would be as well if you directed your strictures to the letter carrier over whom alone you possess control' and by doing which you would establish for the General Post Office a character of impartiality and fair play.

James Burke *vs* J.M. Fallon

Despite his vindication by no less a literary gentleman than Anthony Trollope and the obvious jubilation this provoked, within a week or so of that hearing, poor James Burke was in the witness stand in Athlone Court House giving evidence in a case concerning his assault by Mr J.M. Fallon. As you might have guessed, the assault arose out of an altercation concerning the mis-delivery of letters.

Burke gave evidence that on 9 December he had a letter directed to a Mr W. O'Fallon and that 'the boy in the office' told him to show it to Mr Joseph Fallon. In the course of trying to establish the identity of the person to whom the letter was addressed, he showed it to Mr J.M. Fallon. Fallon took the letter from him, called a witness, and following him said that the letter was not for him (Dr Fallon) but for Councillor Fallon.

On the twentieth of the month, a further letter was received directed to a Mr Fallon. Burke decided to show it to a number of Fallons to see which of them might claim it as their own, and if there was a dispute about it he intended returning it to the post office. He claimed, however, that Fallon 'seized him, struck him, pushed him into Stanford's and forced the letter from him', and then excited a mob against him. He even claimed that Fallon had a 'parcel of dogs so well tutored' against him that if they were brought into court they would be 'heedless of the rest' present and rush at him. At this remark there was laughter in the court and Mr Fallon asked the court for permission to bring in the dogs!

John Stanford also gave evidence in which he stated that Burke had not voted for Mr Ferrall in the last election. However, he felt that there was no enmity on that account. On the contrary he claimed that he wished him well, but claimed that he could not speak for others; as far as he was concerned the only opposition to Mr Burke was that he was unable to read the letters which he was sent about to distribute.

The case against Fallon was dismissed and judging from the lack of any further evidence, we must assume that James Burke made a wise move and decided on a career change.

21

Remembering
Pearse Street

I met an old Athlonian during the week, visiting her hometown, who asked me whether I could recall Pearse Street as a busy and thriving business street. I assured her that I could and as a result, I thought I would allow myself to indulge in a little bit of nostalgia.

Through an accident of birth, or perhaps divine intervention, I was born in Dublin, in The Coombe, in the heart of the Liberties – but I am definitely not a Dub! I have since spent fifty years trying to make up for my absence from Athlone at that crucial point in my existence. The town I remember from the early 1960s was very different from the sprawling neon-lit town of today. The hustle and bustle of childhood that I most remember was the convoy of navy and maroon prams and go-cars (the term 'buggy' hadn't yet been applied to this form of transport) which lined up outside the shops. I'm sure I babbled at every other baby in Athlone as I sucked the pimples off my Lincoln Creams outside Maguire's in Mardyke Street or Lipton's in Custume Place, while my mother bought her groceries. Apart from prams and go-cars, the next most widespread form of transport was undoubtedly the humble pedal-cycle. Flotillas of sturdy black bikes made their way to and from schools, the army barracks and Gentex. Cars were still relatively scarce in those days and the arrival of a new car in town was a source of wonder.

A view of Pearse Street in the late 1950s.

A view of Pearse Street and Barrack Street, *c.* 1960.

Journey into Connaught

I was reared on the Leinster side of Athlone and my journeys into Connaught were few and far between. That is, of course, until I went to National School, when I opted for my schooling on 'the far side', in the Dean Kelly Memorial School on the Batteries.

As a child, crossing the trembling, clattering Bailey bridge was either a frightening ordeal or a great adventure, depending on one's state of mind. The reward for crossing the bridge was usually a visit to the market, which then consisted of purely local produce. How I loved to watch the tumbling vats of eels, the hobbled fowl huddled under the carts, or the spancelled kid goats shivering beneath the castle walls. To me, the squirming of the eel, the cackle of the fowl and the half-hearted bleating of the kid were all a celebration of life. And so the myth continued, until one day I watched the deftness of the skinner's knife as he removed a kid skin as simply as a mother would remove a child's coat. Then I realised that the presence of all this life was only a prelude to death. It was then the market lost its magic for me, and at just seven years of age I turned vegetarian.

Pearse Street

Pearse Street, known to the older folk as King Street, had a life of its own. Then it too died, but thankfully it has now risen, phoenix-like from the ashes. Those who have taken the brave decision to modernise, renovate and indeed to open new businesses here deserve our thanks and our custom. Once more, Pearse Street looks set to become a bustling street adding to the attraction of the Left Bank. But Pearse Street is changed so utterly from my school days that little more than the gradient of the street remains the same. The Garda barracks then, as now, stood at the foot of the hill and I remember the visits of the school attendance officer to the classroom. Garda Maurice Tobin was a friendly soul who could turn on the tough-man act when confronting a school truant or when checking our bicycles for roadworthiness. Coming home from school we would meet the Gardaí out on their beat and know that all was well with the world.

When I think back, I remember the genteel Misses Fallers, standing at their doorway and asking the time of passersby – and to think that their ancestors were clockmakers! I can still hear the metallic rush of the barber next door as he sharpens his razor on the strap, awaiting another customer. Outside Newell's a horse and cart is tied to the 'No Parking' sign, and if I'm lucky the alley door will be open and I will hear the twittering of all those exotic birds, from hummingbirds to zebra finches.

I recall the never-ending flow of people coming and going from the surgeries of both doctors and dentists, and the queues in Naylor's chemist shop; Dan O'Connell with his sweet shop on one side of the street, and Frank Egan's men's shop on the other, and the bold Paddy Hegarty saving soles to beat the band. How the years have changed this street, almost beyond recognition. I lament all the shops that have gone but none as much as Lyster's (locally pronounced 'Lester's'), for here I made many friends. Each department had its own friendly staff, and even as a child I was always sure of first-class attention if I sought out Mrs Harvey or Mrs Browne. Entering Lyster's was entering another world, with so many departments, yards, lofts and levels – and seemingly great potential for a young lad like myself to get lost. Entering Lyster's was always an adventure. I can still hear the busy whirr of the overhead carrier for change and the guttural tones of old Mr McCrea as he hands me back a few coppers in change, and see a young Jimmy O'Connor writing out a docket for the yard.

Bank of Ireland, Pearse Street, 1961.

A Thruppeny Ice Cream

Whenever I pass the launderette and see the dirty linen of the town being washed whiter than white, I lament the passing of Patsy Murray's shop. That a new generation of children is growing up in Athlone without ever knowing the magic that was Murray's seems a shame to say the least. Oh, what a treat it was to go in and look at the array of toys, to strap on a gun and holster set and practise a 'quick draw' reflected in a Fry's Cream mirror while the sisters scooped the delicious ice cream into the waiting cones – nothing could ever rival it.

New Developments

As a local historian, I am used to looking at Athlone down through the ages. I can empathise with those who lived here in the last century. However, at the moment the town is developing at an alarming rate – at a rate far greater than any of us would have predicted. I'm saddened that, despite the efforts of all concerned, dirt and squalor are still the problems that they were a century ago, and I hope we will soon be able to get our act together on that score. But don't get me wrong, I still love Athlone with a passion which sometimes defies logic. To me, to be ostracised from the town I wasn't born in would be as great a punishment as I could ever imagine. Yet sometimes it is good to remember Athlone as it was then – a large town – and to consider it now as a fledgling city, ready to fulfil its role as the natural capital of the midlands and a place we can be proud to call our own.

22

The Athlone
Felt Hat Industry

Many authorities state that the manufacture of felt hats was the most important industry in eighteenth-century Athlone, but it took an inquiry from a Swift scholar in Germany to focus my full attention on the matter. Last June I had a letter from a Professor in Westfälische Wilhelms-Universität in Münster, Germany asking the question: were Athlone felt hats a household name in Dean Swift's lifetime and would his readers have immediately identified with the product concerned?

In attempting to answer this query, it seemed to be a case of 'which came first the chicken or the egg', because in the past the evidence we have used to prove the importance of the Athlone felt hats was that they were mentioned by no less a literary figure than Dean Jonathan Swift himself! Jonathan Swift's reference to Athlone felt hats is contained in his celebrated *Proposal for the Universal Use of Irish Manufacture*, first published in 1720:

> I think it needless to exhort the clergy to follow this good example because in a little time, those among them who are so unfortunate to have had their birth and education in this country, will think themselves abundantly happy when they can afford Irish crape, and an Athlone hat; and as to the others I shall not presume to direct them. I have indeed seen the present Archbishop of Dublin clad from head to foot in our own manufacture; and yet, under the rose be it

spoken, his Grace deserves as good a gown as any prelate in Christendom.

Acknowledged expert on Irish dress, Mairead Dunlevy of the National Museum of Ireland, in describing fashionable dress in Ireland during the period 1700-70, writes:

> As men wore wigs, they often carried, rather than wore, their hats. Beaver and coney were the most fashionable fabrics but apart from that, Irish felt-makers and hatters advertised 'all sorts of fine hats, Carolinas, hats for keeping out the rain with Athlone felts and all other sorts fine and coarse'. Athlone hats were particularly popular and referred to regularly. Hats varied in shape and style according to the height of the round crown and the manner in which the brim was 'cocked' or turned up.

So what was this felt made from? There is a suggestion that wool and rabbit fur may have been combined to make Athlone felt. The felting process has been known since antiquity, and felted fabrics were probably made before woven fabrics. Non-woven felt was produced from a matted sheet of tangled wool, hair or fur. Heat, combined with pressure, moisture and other chemical action, causes the shrinkage of the wool fibres. A felt hat is usually made from wool fibres, soft fur, or a combination of both. In modern felt hat making, pieces of wool or fur are formed around a cone in a thin layer and then placed in hot water. The water shrinks the layer into a piece of felt. The felt is then stretched into the rough shape of the hat and then placed on a head block. A blocking machine shapes the crown and brim, and the hat is washed in cold water to set its shape. The hat is then sandpapered to give it a smooth finish, and the brim is trimmed to size.

In taking a closer look at the history of the felt industry in Ireland, other eighteenth-century references arise which confirm the fact that the Athlone hat was indeed a superior product and that Athlone was noted as a centre of excellence in felt manufacture. Molyneaux, in his *Journey to Connaught, 1709*, in describing his journey through Athlone states:

> Left Moat with Staples in ye coach about 9 a clock. Came in three hours, thro' indifferent coach roads, wild sheepwalks, and scrubby hills and bogs, to Athlone, which is a handsome large town, scituated on ye noble river ye Shannon. Here we saw ye miserable ruins of ye castle, which was some years ago blown up, ye magazine of powder there kept taking fire by accident. Here are a horse and foot barrack and some good brass and iron ordinance. The town is famous for ye manufacture of felts, which are sold from 2 to 4 shillings price.

The Royal Hospital in Kilmainham was built over 300 years ago for 'decay'd souldiers', and when it was handed over to the State in 1984 an account of the allowances given to the Kilmainham pensioners was given in the *Sunday Tribune*. Unfortunately, we do not have a date for the account, but it probably dates to around 1700. The old soldiers were given a weekly allowance of 2*d* worth of tobacco each. Every two years they got a scarlet coat and a waistcoat, and every year a pair of breeches, an Athlone hat with gold lace, a pair of blue worsted stockings, a pair of shoes, a cravat, two shirts and two linen caps.

Evidence that the industry was already in decline may be gleaned from the writings of another great Irishman, Bishop George Berkeley, who, in his publication *The Querist* (originally published in three parts between 1735 and 1737), posed the following question as Query 533, 'Whether we had not some years since a manufacture of hats at Athlone, and of earthenware at Arklow, and what became of these manufactures?'

The Querist was intended to make the people think about various questions of public interest without laying down any dogmatic answers. However, by posing the question, Berkeley implies that by 1735 the industry which had been so highly praised by Swift was already in decline.

Today, a small laneway in Athlone granting access to the Shannon between AIB Bank and the town bridge is properly known as Hatters' Lane, although in practice the name is seldom used. The name is used, however, in several eighteenth-century deeds and appears on the first Ordnance Survey map of 1838. This, and other evidence, suggests that the felt hat manufacturing was carried out in the town centre, convenient to the River Shannon.

The Earliest Recorded Hatters

The earliest recorded Athlone hatters were Randal and John Acton, who were already well settled here by 1684, and George Shore, a Quaker who is first mentioned in 1687. George Shore was imprisoned in Mullingar Gaol in 1671 for nonconformity and for refusing to pay tithes. The Actons were the leading family of Athlone hatters and most likely the people who earned Athlone the reputation for the quality of its hats. The Feltmakers' Company of Dublin was incorporated by royal charter in 1667 and the Actons obviously joined as journeymen felt makers at the earliest opportunity. The usual condition of admission of journeymen was that they could prove their service in the provinces for seven years. The Actons were leading merchants in Athlone; they signed an address to King James II in 1684 and Randal Acton is listed as a warden of the Feltmakers' Company in 1693, surely a rare distinction for a provincial felt maker. In 1698, Randal Acton sent a petition to the Irish parliament seeking protection for the Athlone felt-making industry from the attempts which the English manufacturers were only too successfully making to crush and extirpate it. Subsequently, other members of the Acton family attained the position of Master of the Feltmakers' Company, presumably in recognition of their contribution to the industry. Thomas was sworn in as Master in 1702 and John in 1704. When the serving Master, Edward Nowlan, left the company in September 1719, Thomas Acton was elected to fill the vacancy for the rest of that year. The historian G.T. Stokes states that the Actons continued to live and work as felt makers in Athlone until the close of the eighteenth century at least.

Dr John Burgess, in his papers held in the Aidan Heavey Public Library in Athlone, identifies the following felt makers and hatters in Athlone:

Athlone Felt Makers

1684 Randall Acton, Strand Street, Warden, Feltmakers' Co., 1693
1684 John Acton, Master, Feltmakers' Co., 1704
1687 George Shoare, Custume Place
1702 Thomas Acton, Master Feltmakers' Co., 1702, 1719.
1716 Robert Boswell, Church Street, Member, Feltmakers' Co.
1716 James Cuff, Hatters' Lane
1716 John Roe, Strand Street
1716 John Howell, Strand Street
1720 Thomas Dillon, Preaching Lane
1720 James Mulligan, Hatters' Lane
1720 Richard Price, Stapleshill Lane
1724 George Cuff
1727 John Boswell
1729 James Blyth, Northgate Street
1731 Edward Howe, Hatters' Lane
1739 Thomas Craig (also a town bailiff)
1744 Robert Crosthwaite, Bonavalley
1753 William Naghten, Irishtown

Athlone Hatters

1706 Edward Hargadon (or Hargid), Member, Feltmakers' Co.
1707 Roger McLoughlin, do

1716 Francis McCabe, Hatters' Lane, do
1720 Thady Kelly, do
1729 Peter McLoughlin, do
1745 Thomas Gray
1738 Henry Hill, Northgate Street
1752 Robert Hill, do
1784 Robert Connor, Bridge Street

While Robert Connor resided at Bridge Street, we know from the Registry of Deeds that he also held four cabins in Hatters' Lane, on the south side, and that his felt manufactory was on the north side of the lane near the Shannon, where he also held a small house and garden.

Hopefully the foregoing note will help to convince even the most sceptical Swift scholar that the Athlone felt hat was indeed a most desirable addition to any gentleman's wardrobe. In July 1733, Thomas Smith, Hatter on the Blind Quay, Dublin, advertised in the *Dublin Evening Post* that he could 'supply Athlone Felt Hats at reasonable rates'. Without a doubt, Athlone hats were the preferred headgear of the Irish gentleman for most of the seventeenth century. By 1828, the Feltmakers' Company of Dublin issued a notice to the public, stating that in consequence of the great rise in the price of materials for manufacturing hats, it would in future be quite out of the power of the trade to sell hats at their former prices.

The Last Days of the Industry

Rising prices sounded the death knell for the Athlone felt hat industry. Some of the families involved had noted the changing trends and had opted to diversify and invest in other, more lucrative, industries (most notably the Boswell's, who became brewers). Some of the smaller players moved into allied trades, with a few becoming cordwainers, and inevitably, I suppose, a few mad hat-

ters★ persisted in their trade. The Athlone-born historian Dr G.T.
Stokes (1843-1898), in a footnote to his article on 'Athlone in the
seventeenth century' written in 1890, states, 'The trade did not
die out till living memory. I myself remember some few makers
of felt hats and their shops.'

The old Tholsel or Market House, which stood in Custume
Place facing down into Northgate Street, was dismantled in
around 1836. In 1894, local historian James Hill wrote an article
in the *Westmeath Independent* recalling the Tholsel:

> It was an old pentagon [*sic*] building, three stories high, built
> in 1703 ... It was placed where the most traffic was held and
> being in a line with the old bridge was a great obstruction to
> the thoroughfare. It had a pointed bell shaped tower, a bell at
> present in St Mary's church and on the top a peculiar shaped
> cross ... a corridor went around the bottom floor, used on
> market days where felt hats, boots etc. were exposed for sale ...

These two references indicate that the last Athlone hatters survived until the mid-nineteenth century at least. Today, Athlone
hats are an almost forgotten commodity, depending on a few literary references for their reputation. But who knows, even at this
late stage some enterprising Athlonian may well be inspired by
Swift or Berkeley to reinvent the Athlone felt hat!

★ *The phrase 'As mad as a hatter' goes back far beyond Lewis Carroll's*
Alice's Adventures in Wonderland. *The term is used to describe someone who is insane or crazy. It is widely believed that it originates from the
fact that in the manufacture of felt hats, hatters used nitrate of mercury,
exposure to which caused both mental and physical symptoms which were
sometimes interpreted as madness. So who knows, perhaps we had plenty
of 'mad hatters' in seventeenth-century Athlone!*

23

Dirty Old Town: Some Less-Than Flattering Accounts of Athlone

I am constantly on the lookout for early printed accounts of the town of Athlone. Unfortunately, whenever I find them they are usually less than flattering. In the 1830s and '40s, among the several visitors to Athlone who left us written accounts of their impressions of the town are: the novelist Maria Edgeworth, the German journalist and commentator Herr J. Venedy, and the famous Irish antiquarian John O'Donovan, who travelled the length and breadth of the country in search of material for the first Ordnance Survey of Ireland in the 1830s.

Maria Edgeworth in Athlone

Maria Edgeworth (1767-1849) is best remembered today as a novelist and author of such works as *Castle Rackrent* (1800) and two series entitled 'Tales of Fashionable Life' of which *Ormond* and *The Absentee* are perhaps the best remembered. Maria was English born but her family moved to Ireland to live in Edgeworthstown, County Longford when she was fifteen years old. Maria Edgeworth was a remarkable woman and has been the subject of various studies, including one by the Athlone-born writer and critic Dr Patrick Murray. *Castle Rackrent* was a ground-breaking novel, and even Sir Walter Scott acknowledged his debt to its petite author. Maria was very close to, and influenced by,

Maria Edgeworth (1767-1849), British author. A steel engraving after a painting by Alonzo Chappel (1828-1887). (© Mary Evans)

her father. She collaborated with him in writing a number of books, including his *Essays on Practical Education.* She assisted with the rearing of her twenty-one siblings and taught with him in a school which he established on the family estate. Maria's earliest writings included educational works and moral tales written for young readers.

Her description of Athlone comes from a rather unusual source, as it was included in a long letter which she sent to her youngest brother, Michael Pakenham Edgeworth, who was serving with the East India Company in 1834. The letter refers to a tour through Connemara in which Maria was accompanied by Sir Culling and Lady Culling Smith. While excerpts from this letter have been published over the years, the full text did not appear in print until 1950, when Harold Edgeworth Butler edited it and published it in a limited edition as *Tour in Connemara and the Martins of Ballinahinch.* The following piece describes her passage through Athlone and progress westwards following a great sheep fair at Ballinasloe. The original letter was dated 8 March, 1834:

Of Athlone I have nothing to say but what you may learn from the Gazetteer except that while we were waiting in the antiquated inn there, while horses were changing, I espied a print hanging smoked over the chimney-piece, which to my connoisseur eyes seemed marvellously good, and upon my own judgement I proposed for it to the landlady, and bought it for five shillings (frame excepted) and when I had it out of the frame I found my taste and judgement gloriously justified. It was from a picture of Van Dyke's *The Death of Belisarius* and here it is now hanging up in the library, the admiration of all beholders, Barry Fox, above all. [Major Barry Fox, of Foxhall, County Longford was a cousin of Maria's.] But to proceed. It was no easy matter to get out of Athlone, for at the entrance of the old fashioned, narrowest of narrow bridges we found ourselves wedged and blocked by drays and sheep reaching a mile at least; men cursing and swearing in Irish and English; sheep baaing and so terrified that the shepherds were in transports of fear, brandishing their crooks at the postillions in turn slashing their whips on the impassive backs of the sheep. The cocked gold hat of an officer appeared on horseback in the midst, and there was silence from all but the baaing sheep. He bowed to us ladies, or to our carriage and four, and assured us he would see us safe out, but that it would be a work of time. And while this work of time was going on, one pushed his way from behind, between sheep and the wheel on my side of the carriage, and putting in his head called to me: 'Miss Edgeworth, if you are in it, my master's in town and will be with you directly almost, with his best compliments ...'

I cannot tell you – and if I could, you would think I exaggerated – how many hours we were in getting through the next ten miles, the road being continually covered with sheep, thick as wool could pack, all coming from the sheep fair of Ballinasloe, which, to Sir Culling's intense mortification, we now found had taken place the previous day.

There are several interesting aspects of this description. It would be impossible to guess which Athlone inn the party had visited, but perhaps it was Miss Gray's, as we know that at that period it was run by a landlady as opposed to a landlord. The fact that men were cursing in Irish as well as English is in itself interesting, and, of course, the description of the old Elizabethan bridge of Athlone towards the end of its life captures the horrific scene which was part and parcel of market day in Athlone.

Herr Venedy's View of Athlone

In 1843, Herr J. Venedy, a German admirer of Daniel O'Connell's who spent a year following The Liberator around the country, arrived in Athlone to attend the great Repeal meeting which was held at Summerhill, Athlone on 18 June. His original account, which was written in German, was translated into English by William Bernard McCabe and published by William J. Duffy of Dublin in 1844. It is called *Ireland and the Irish in the Repeal Year, 1843* and it is a very scarce work. The following description of the town of Athlone is taken from pages 54 and 55.

> When I approached the town my human sympathies were, however, soon again excited, for here as elsewhere I could not stir a step, without stumbling over the shattered remains of decayed mansions, and the ruins of desolate huts. Aye, I even encountered so many of them, that at last the thought suggested itself, that these might be regarded not so much as evidences of the general misery of the people, as evidences of their customs and manners. But let us pause before we give judgement. This much, however, is certain; I saw new houses built near to the ruins of the old; I saw that the stone used in the new was of the same material as that which had been employed in the erection of the old, and yet the peasantry never seemed to think of appropriating for the new that which was at their hands, and

thus lay uselessly encumbering the ground. Upon reaching the town, I inquired my way to a bookseller's shop, because I had unfortunately packed up in Dublin my map of Ireland. I soon discovered, that in Athlone, a town with ten thousand inhabitants – having too, a fortress, and a large garrison of soldiers, that there was nothing which even resembled a bookshop. There is even no public school in Athlone. The children are sent to private schools, or they go to none at all. Whilst, then, I was thinking over the many evil results that must follow from the want of libraries and schools, I had soon a proof that there was a printing press in the town, for I perceived in the street an old hateful-looking, dirty woman, bawling out, in a frightful screaming voice, a song which had been composed, set to music, and printed in Athlone, to the honour of O'Connell.

As I passed over the bridge I encountered a picture which would be worthy of the greatest master. In a corner sat an old beggar woman in rags, and squatted in the pure oriental fashion. With her left hand she held a little pipe in her mouth, whilst her right, outstretched, rested on her knees, waiting for alms. There was the bloom of two little red Barsdorf apples on her cheeks, the eyes were half closed, and the mouth, with a friendly, perfectly contented smile, puffed forth a thin cloud of tobacco smoke into the air. If I could paint a perfect picture of 'happiness', then would I take that old beggar-woman, precisely as she sat before me, for my model.

Herr Venedy was on a whistle-stop tour, but nonetheless his observations are interesting. Athlone was frequently without a bookshop or a library but both of these services appeared and disappeared at fairly regular intervals in Victorian Athlone. By 1843, there were public schools (National Schools) in St Mary's parish, at Ankers Bower and in the Coosan district, but it was not until 1845 that St Peter's parish had a National School at Deerpark Road. While there was the Ranelagh Endowed School, a private school run by the Church of Ireland, the notion of secondary education in Athlone did not materialise generally until the arrival of the sisters of La Sainte Union and the Marist Brothers, both in 1884.

The printing press that Herr Venedy referred to was that of Mr J. Thompson, who founded two early Athlone newspapers: *The Athlone Independent (or Midland Telegraph)* which flourished from 1833–36 and the short-lived *Athlone Conservative Advocate and Ballinasloe Reporter*, which ran from June to September 1837. The earlier newspaper was printed at his offices in Irishtown. Two earlier printers in Athlone were Ephraim Proctor, who founded *The Athlone Chronicle* around 1770, and Daniel Daly of High Street, who was also a newspaper proprietor. Mr Daly occupied the premises later occupied by Roe & Son, tailor.

The nineteenth century was a golden age for recording the history, topography and geography of Ireland. Many early Irish manuscript sources were edited and brought before a new and enthusiastic audience, and standards of research were improving all the time. It was a time of great Irish scholarship, and high among those scholars was John O'Donovan (1809-1861).

John O'Donovan was born in Slieverue, County Kilkenny in 1809, but the premature death of his father took him to live in Dublin in 1817. His uncle Peter, who was his guardian, gave him a great love for the Irish language and culture, and after that he became something of a self-taught scholar. In 1826, as a callow youth, he went to work in the Irish Record Office under the watchful eye of James Hardiman, who was later to write *Hardiman's History of Galway*. In 1829, he joined the Historical Department of the Irish Ordnance Survey under another great Irish scholar, George Petrie. Here he was to list 62,000 Irish place names and record the origins of these names, the genealogies of the great Irish families and all the extant knowledge he could gather on the archaeological remains of Ireland. His partner in this venture was an equally distinguished scholar: Eugene O'Curry.

John O'Donovan's View of Athlone

In the course of his all too short life, O'Donovan was responsible for publishing several major works, including a translation of an Irish dictionary, a grammar of the Irish language, *Tribes and customs of Hy-Many, commonly called O'Kelly country, Tribes and customs of Hy-Fiachrach, commonly called O'Dowda country, Leabhar na gCeart (The Book of Rights)*, and his seven-volume edition of the *Annals of the Four Masters*. However, one of his most important legacies was perhaps unintentional. While out on fieldwork for the Ordnance Survey, he wrote copious letters to George Petrie. These were edited by Fr Michael O'Flanagan (a native of County Roscommon) in fifty typescript volumes and give valuable insights into matters of antiquarian interest nationwide, as well as glimpses into the character of the author.

We can be sure that he never expected this correspondence to come into the public domain. In May 1837, he found himself in Athlone in a rather impecunious condition. In a letter to head office dated 27 May 1837 he states, 'We have arrived here at three o'clock this morning and obtained three hours rest. O'Conor is knocked up, but I am getting more and more vigorous every day, from which I infer that sedentary habits throw my constitution out of its natural element.' He continues by explaining that he was 'able to bring to Athlone five shillings of the five pounds you sent me', and laments the fact that they can't stay in one place for longer and that they can't afford to stay in public houses. He confesses to working 'eleven hours every day (Sunday as well as the rest) since I left Dublin' in the hopes of finishing his fieldwork before winter. However, it is in the colourful postscript to this letter that he sums up his view of Athlone:

> Athlone is the ugliest town in Europe! Its bridge is scandalous. I hope the Shannon will sweep it away to make them build a dacent one. Such a confusion (chaos) of women, Connaughtmen, horses, asses, potatoes, soldiers, peelers would

almost make one swear that there is no order in nature. This is market day.

Of course, apart from this brief but scathing account of Athlone, John O'Donovan also left us extremely useful source material on Athlone and Westmeath. This is to be found in the Ordnance Survey Letters (Westmeath) and the Field Name Books for the county, which are still the first port of call for many people researching the history and archaeology of the county. The death of John O'Donovan at fifty-two years of age robbed Ireland of one of its finest scholars.

Fr Conmee: 'Old Times in the Barony'

One cannot help thinking that Fr Conmee had probably seen John O'Donovan's remarks on Athlone before he wrote his own wonderful account of market day in the town. John Conmee was born in Glanduff in the parish of St John's on Christmas Day, 1847. Later his family moved to Boyle, but John was educated in Dublin, first in Castleknock and later in Clongowes Wood. In 1867, he joined the Jesuit Order, having completed his secondary education with them. He entered the order at Milltown Park, Dublin and later studied in England and on the continent, before returning to Ireland in 1881 to be ordained by the legendary Archbishop Croke of Cashel.

After ordination he was appointed as Prefect of Studies at Clongowes and four years later he was made rector of the college. During his stint as Rector of Clongowes, from 1885-91, he was to come into contact with the young James Joyce – indeed he is credited with influencing the decision to have Joyce accepted into Belvedere College. James Joyce obviously remembered the various acts of kindness of Conmee with gratitude; he later immortalised him as the rector in *Portrait of the Artist* and gave him a very significant role in *Ulysses*.

Fr Conmee was the author of a thoroughly charming booklet, first published by the Catholic Truth Society of Ireland in 1895. It has been reprinted by CTSI, and Sean Day of Carraig Books in Blackrock, County Dublin, produced a facsimile edition in 1976. This booklet, called 'Old times in the Barony', relates to the Barony of Athlone in County Roscommon. It is one of a handful of scarce but interesting pamphlets on Athlone which no local history collection would be complete without. His description of those coming to the market in Athlone is a charming account of rural life in late Victorian times:

On market days, for instance, how interesting the great vehicular procession that wended its easy-going way to Luainford [Athlone]! What a display of 'dray' and 'kish' and 'crate' – those rustic argosies freighted with the simple merchandise of the homestead and the field. Sometimes it would be a farmer seated with praise-worthy self-denial on the narrow shaft of his cart, hard by his horse's tail, who drove along a high crate, which was little less than a menagerie of domestic live stock. Over the top would leer the loutish visage and lolling tongue of a calf – through the bars would peer the bewildered face of a sheep – while a substratum of little pigs – 'bonnuvs' in the local speech – would make their presence known by squealing protests against the joltings of the road which huddled them so unceremoniously together. Or again, it would be the open dray, in the midst of which Barny would recognise the good woman of the household, wrapped in an ample cloak, and surrounded by the fruits of many a month of patient industry – the neatly covered crocks of butter, the different baskets that contained the barn-door fowl in every stage of development, from the new-laid egg to the 'clockin' hen – the produce of the spinning wheel and the knitting needle – and certain verdant bundles of cabbage plants for the growth of which the Barony enjoyed a distinguished reputation among horticultural cognoscenti even as far as Banagher and Mullingar.

24

The Great John L. Sullivan

Reading Michael Heavey's book *The May Morning Dew: Ireland and the American Civil War* reminded me about two of the greatest Irish-American boxers of the nineteenth century, both of whom had local roots. These two, who famously locked horns in an epic contest in Richburg in 1889, were John L. Sullivan and Jake Kilraine.

The forerunner to the modern sport of boxing (under the Queensbury Rules) was 'prizefighting', in which two opponents fought for an agreed stake plus a share in the bets. The prizefighting era, which was governed (since 1839) by the London Prize Ring rules, lead to fights of savage length. The number of rounds was not preset but depended on the physical endurance of the fighters. The great John L. Sullivan was one of the links between the old style bare-knuckle 'prizefighting' and the modern gloved boxing contests.

The Boston Strongboy

John Lawrence Sullivan was born on 15 October 1858 in the Roxbury district of Boston, Massachusetts. He was the son of Mike Sullivan, a builder's labourer (or hod carrier) from Abeydorney County Kerry. His mother, Catherine Kelly, was born on a farm at Curramore, Kiltoom, just outside Athlone.

Both his parents had emigrated to America in the immediate aftermath of the Famine. John's father was no more than 5ft 3ins in height and was known for his combative nature; he was also a hard drinker and unfortunately John inherited both these traits. His fine stature, we are told, was inherited from his mother. John L. Sullivan stood 5ft 10ins tall and throughout his career weighed in at anywhere between 190lb and 229lb. His mother hoped that John would become a priest, and enrolled him in Boston College, but his sojourn there was brief. Instead of opting for a career in the Church, the young John L. worked briefly on the buildings, before embarking on a career as a plumber's apprentice. This career choice was also short-lived; we are told he broke his employer's jaw in a dispute over work practices and he then embarked on a career as a tinsmith.

At an early age he showed prowess as a boxer but despite his success his father was constantly belittling his ability. One biographer quotes his father, 'So you think ye're a great fighter d'ye? Bedad there's men in ould Oirland could smash you in pieces with one punch.' Undeterred by his father's taunts, or perhaps determined to prove him wrong, John L. Sullivan started to fight professionally when he was twenty years old. Four years later, on 7 February 1882, he fought Paddy Ryan, the Thurles-born Heavyweight Champion, in Mississippi City. The fight, which was a bare-knuckle contest, ended in a knockout for Sullivan. He emerged victorious, with the Heavyweight Championship title, and launched a major boxing career.

John L. Sullivan was the first boxing superstar. He was an extrovert showman who was prepared to tour the country, throwing down the gauntlet and taking on all comers. The challenge was to go four rounds with the champion and the reward was $1,000. It is said that up to fifty men took up the challenge but only one lasted the pace.

'The Boston Strongboy', as he was known, held the heavyweight title for ten years, until he was matched with 'Gentleman Jim' Corbett. It was John L. Sullivan who finally made the move that aligned professional fighters on the side of the Queensbury Rules. He did so not out of a sense of sport, but because he felt he could not afford to do otherwise. John L. lived hard and fought hard. The years of high living had started to take their toll long before he lost his title, when knocked out by Corbett in the twenty-first round.

Sullivan *vs* Kilraine

The last significant fight of the bare-knuckle era was fought in Richburg, Mississippi on 8 July 1889 and it was the subject of a special supplement of the *New York Illustrated News*. The opponents were John L. Sullivan and Jake Kilraine. The fight was of epic proportions; it lasted seventy-five rounds until John L. eventually brought down Kilraine. By a strange quirk of fate, both boxers had local ties, indeed it has been claimed that they might have been related to one another. They both certainly had strong Athlone connections.

John L. Visits Athlone

In 1910, John L. Sullivan visited Athlone, accompanied by his wife, and the couple stayed in the Prince of Wales Hotel. The former Heavyweight Champion had come in search of his roots. His mother was a Kelly from Curramore, his sister, it seems, was married to a Killian from Drum, and there was also a relationship with a Lennon family in the same locality.

Interviewed in the 1960s, the late Mr James Galvin of Connaught Street, who was then one of the oldest men in Athlone, recalled that his father 'and half of the town' had gone to Denis Connell's in O'Connell Street to shake the hand of John L. Sullivan, the man who shook the world.

John L. Sullivan certainly earned his place in the annals of boxing. While he is generally considered to have been a World

Heavyweight Champion, some boxing historians regard him as a US Champion only. Regardless of his status as a champion, it is estimated that he earned more than $1,000,000 in the ring.

Sullivan Turns to Theatricals

Ever the showman, John L. Sullivan turned to the stage after his retirement from the ring. The *Irish Weekly Independent* of 8 February 1902 reported:

> The ex-champion pugilist now on stage is said to be making a financial success in his *Uncle Tom's Cabin* tour in which he plays the part of the ruffianly Legree the slave-driver. He now weighs 280lbs. He does not like being the villain of the piece. The hisses worry him.

Sullivan spent as much as he earned. He was fond of the high life and his drinking had become a problem. In a surprise move, he took the pledge and turned from drink to a temperance lecturer. As a reformed character, he was reconciled with his wife and the pair lived out their retirement on a small farm outside Boston. Apart from occasional celebrity appearances, John L. Sullivan then lived the quiet life. He was on very good terms with the US president Theodore 'Teddy' Roosevelt.

John L. Sullivan visited Ireland at least twice; once in 1887, when he visited Waterford, Cork and Limerick, and again in 1910 (when he visited Athlone) on a vaudeville tour of Britain and Ireland.

John L. Sullivan died on 2 February 1918. The streets were lined with crowds weeping and mourning the passing of this colossus as his coffin was carried to Calvary Cemetery. At the graveside, the priest paid a stirring tribute to the man and in particular to his victory over his greatest enemy – the demon drink.

25

St Peter's Port

When considering the history of Athlone, and the place of the Shannon in the life of the town, there can be no more interesting story than that of St Peter's Port. This port or harbour was once crucial in the life of Athlone but is no longer. Older folk who remember the gateway into St Gabriel's Laundry, attached to St Peter's Convent of Mercy, will recall the crude carvings which once stood above the archway, and the stones on either side of the gate inscribed with the following unusual couplet:

> O May not Satan's agents enter,
> Will o'Wisp and Jack the Printer.

Over the years, these stones posed an enigma to the curious passerby. Visitors often enquired as to the origins of the stones, but at the time they were erected everyone knew exactly who the two characters in question were.

The Walter Scott Connection

In 1833, when he was quartered in Athlone, Capt. Walter Scott, son of the celebrated novelist of the same name, wrote to his father, and in the course of his letter mentioned the couplet which he had discovered on an old gateway in the town. A few weeks later, Sir Walter Scott wrote back to his son, sending him a copy of his most recently published novel accompanied by fifteen pages of a manuscript closely written to prove that the inscription must read 'Jack the Painter'. Scott went on to say that after considerable research, he had concluded that Will o'Wisp was one of the Confederates. Jack the Painter had been hanged at Edinburgh but had once visited Ireland. Scott put forward the supposition that he must have visited Athlone and that he had 'made himself so notorious at Athlone by his villanies and vices as to cause this memento of him to be placed in the gate of the town'.

We will see that Sir Walter Scott was clearly a better novelist than he was a detective. An account from the *Athlone Independent* of 19 March 1833 recalls the visit of Walter Scott the younger to Athlone:

> On Thursday last the headquarters of the 15th Hussars commanded by Major Sir Walter Scott, marched through this town on their route to Longford, the interest excited by the late Court Martial of Captain Watten, the prominent and honourable part taken by the gallant Major on that occasion, the firm soldier-like appearance of the men, and above all the feelings associated with the magic name of 'Walter Scott' brought crowds out to witness their arrival and departure.

It seems that Walter Scott Jr may have dabbled in verse, and one poem, which *The Athlone Times* attributed to him in 1890, almost sixty years after his visit, was certainly not too complimentary to the Irish midlands:

> Loughrea it is a blackguard place,
> To Gort I give my curse.
> Athlone itself is bad enough
> But Ballinasloe is worse.
> I cannot tell which is the worst

They're all so very bad
But of all the towns I ever saw
Bad luck to Kinnegad!

Those Curious Stones

By now we know about the two Walter Scotts but we still don't know about those curious stones at St Peter's Port. Prior to the Shannon Navigation works of the 1840s, full navigation through the Shannon at Athlone was impossible. A century earlier, an interim solution had been to construct a bypass canal on the west side of the town. All goods coming into Athlone by barge were brought ashore at St Peter's Port (in the vicinity of the present docks), where a tax or excise duty was paid, thus giving Excise Street its name.

Sheela-na-Gig and dedication stone of St Peter's Port with the initials 'I.B.' for John Booth.

A deed of 1801 in the name of John Booth describes the St Peter's Port plot (or 'Glasses Plot' as it was then referred to), with the 'antient mansion house thereon, with out-houses, stables, gardens, water-courses and fishings'. On the eastern end of this site, John Booth erected a brewery (known as Booth's Brewery from 1801-1817). John Booth was in business with his brother William in the brewery. It is said that he levied a charge of 2*d* on every boatload that was brought through the port, and for the vehemence with which he collected this tax from everyone he was nicknamed 'Copper-fisted Jack'.

John Booth has been described by Prof. G.T. Stokes as a 'stiff old Puritan of the Baptist persuasion from Kilbeggan or thereabouts, gifted with a good deal of that strong facility of hatred which Puritans at times could display'. He was a member of the family which later became well known through the pneumatic tyre and bicycle industry.

The Quarrel

And so to the origin of the stones. John Booth had a dispute, probably concerning the coveted right of way to the port, with two of his fellow townsmen, Messrs William Sproule and James Potts. William Sproule was a member of an old Quaker family; James Potts was a proprietor of a national newspaper called *Saunder's Newsletter* and his family had several celebrated rows in Dublin. James himself had business interests in Dublin as well as being a tenant in St Peter's Port. The case went to the courts and Booth won, but rather than being content with his victory, he perpetuated his bitter feelings by erecting the offending couplets on either side of the gate to the port. 'Will o' Wisp' referred to William Sproule while 'Jack the Printer' referred to James Potts. It is even said that Booth left instructions in his will that if ever any of his descendants should remove these stones from the gateway that the property should pass out of their hands.

The Reply

The stones caused considerable local interest when they were erected, and according to local tradition the offended parties resorted to a further court case in the hopes of having the stones removed. However, it seems that the court found in favour of old Copper-fisted Jack and he was allowed to retain the stones. The story goes that a local tradesman, Jack Cunniff, composed a reply to the famous couplets, which may have circulated in Athlone as a broadsheet:

> The Apostles' Port would have done as well
> Were you but content
> To have called it so, and few would know
> Which of the twelve you meant.
> St Peter's Port this cannot be
> While faith to scripture's given
> Divines of every age agree
> St Peter's Port is Heaven.
> Who owns it then? It can't be missed
> By those who know they need
> Not Peter blest cursed 'Copper-Fist'
> 'Tis Judas's indeed.

The original stones from St Peter's Port, including the Sheela-na-Gig, the keystone complete with a carved monk's head and the initials 'I.B.', and the two inscribed stones were removed to the museum in Athlone Castle many years ago, when the gateway was dismantled to give greater access to St Gabriel's Laundry. It is believed that the Sheela-na-Gig (a female exhibitionist carving) was removed from the nearby Cluniac Priory by John Booth for safekeeping. These stones, which excited the interest of no less a figure than Sir Walter Scott, are reminders of this port, which was once crucial to the commercial life of Athlone.